The Kingfisher

BOOK OF

1001

QUESTIONS
AND
ANSWERS

BRIDGET AND NEIL ARDLEY

Kingfisher Books

Kingfisher Books, Grisewood & Dempsey Ltd,
Elsley House, 24–30 Great Titchfield Street,
London W1P 7AD

First published in this edition in 1988 by Kingfisher Books
Some of the material in this book was previously
published in *1001 Questions and Answers* in 1981.
Reprinted 1989 (twice), 1990, 1991, 1992 (with revisions)
Copyright © Grisewood & Dempsey Ltd 1988

BRITISH LIBRARY CATALOGUING IN PUBLICATION DATA
Ardley, Bridget
    1001 questions and answers. – 2nd ed.
    1. Curiosities and wonders – Juvenile
literature
    I. Title   II. Ardley, Neil
    032'.02   AG243

    ISBN 0-86272-259-4

Edited by Nan Froman
Cover design: The Pinpoint Design Company
Cover illustration: Ian Jackson
Phototypeset by Southern Positives and Negatives (SPAN),
Lingfield, Surrey
Printed in Italy

CONTENTS

The Universe · 4

The Earth · 20

Animals · 40

THE UNIVERSE

The Big Bang

When did the Universe form?

If the Universe is getting bigger, as astronomers believe, then it must have been smaller in the past. A long time ago, all the galaxies in the Universe would have been squeezed into a small space. Perhaps a great explosion happened, causing the galaxies to spread out through space. This explosion, which is often called the Big Bang, would have happened about 15,000 million years ago.

What is space?

Space is nothing – or almost nothing. It is the space that lies between the Earth and the Moon, between the planets of the Solar System, and between the stars. Space is almost empty. It does not contain any air. A piece of space the size of a house would contain a few atoms of gases and perhaps some specks of dust. Here and there meteoroids and comets move through space.

Where does space begin?

Space begins at the top of the atmosphere. As you go higher, the air gets thinner. At a height of about 160 kilometres the air is so thin that there is virtually none left. This is where space begins.

Is the Earth at the centre of the Universe?

The Universe is everything that exists – all the planets, moons, stars and galaxies (groups of stars) put together. The Universe stretches out in all directions. There may be parts of the Universe that we cannot see through our telescopes, and so we cannot tell whether we are at the centre of the Universe or not.

What holds the Universe together?

The same force that keeps your feet on the ground holds the whole Universe together. This is the force of gravity. Gravity extends through space between planets, between stars and between galaxies. It keeps the planets together in the Solar System and holds the stars together in huge galaxies.

How big is the Universe?

No one knows for sure how big the Universe is. There may be parts of the Universe beyond the reach of our telescopes. Also, astronomers are not sure that light comes from the most distant objects in the Universe in straight lines. The lines could be curved, making the objects closer than they appear to be. However, they could be as much as 15,000 million light years away.

① *The Earth in space*

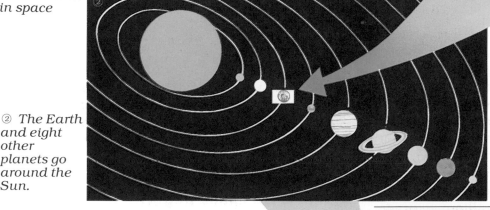

② *The Earth and eight other planets go around the Sun.*

What is a light year?

Distances are so huge between the stars that astronomers do not use kilometres to measure them. Instead they often use light years. A light year is the distance light travels in one year. It is equal to nearly 9.5 million million kilometres.

Will the Universe come to an end?

No one knows the answer to this question. Astronomers believe that the Universe is getting bigger. Perhaps it will go on getting bigger for ever, and will never come to an end. But the expansion of the Universe could be slowing. Perhaps it will stop, and will then begin to get smaller. Eventually, all the galaxies would collide and destroy one another.

③ *Our galaxy is as big as the galaxy at the point of the arrow.*

④ *Our galaxy is only one speck among millions of galaxies.*

Is the Universe getting bigger?

Astronomers can measure the speed with which stars and galaxies are moving. Most of them are moving away from us. The farther away a galaxy is, the faster it appears to be moving away. This means that the Universe is getting bigger.

Planets and the Solar System

Who are the planets named after?

All the planets, except for one, are named after gods and goddesses in Greek or Roman legends. The biggest planet, Jupiter, is named after the Roman king of the gods, for example. The exception is our planet, which we call Earth. This is because the other planets were thought to be in heaven, like the gods, and our planet lay beneath, like the Earth.

What is the difference between a planet and a moon?

A planet is a world that goes around the Sun. A moon is a smaller world that goes around a planet. All except two of the planets have moons. The Earth and Pluto have only one, whereas Jupiter has sixteen. Mercury and Venus have none.

What is the Solar System?

The Solar System is made up of the Sun and all the bodies that go around the Sun. These are the planets and their moons, the asteroids or minor planets, meteoroids and comets. Each moves in a particular path or orbit around the Sun. The Sun's force of gravity holds all these bodies together in the Solar System because it is bigger than they are.

How many planets are there?

The Sun has nine planets. They are Mercury, which is closest to the Sun, and then come Venus, Earth, Mars, Jupiter, Saturn, Uranus, Neptune and finally Pluto. Pluto is usually the most distant planet, but at the moment it is closer to the Sun than Neptune and will be until 1999. We cannot say how many planets there are in the Universe, because other stars almost certainly have planets as well as the Sun, although we cannot see them.

The nine planets of the Solar System and their moons as they go around the Sun

Mercury Venus Earth Mars   *Jupiter*   *Saturn*

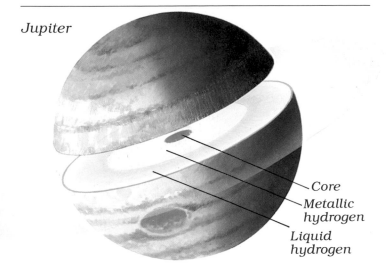

Jupiter

Core
Metallic
hydrogen
Liquid
hydrogen

Which is the biggest planet?

The biggest planet is Jupiter. Its diameter is 142,900 kilometres, more than eleven times the diameter of the Earth. In volume, Jupiter is more than 1300 times the size of the Earth! In fact, Jupiter is so massive that it weighs $2\frac{1}{2}$ times as much as all the other eight planets put together.

Uranus   *Neptune*   *Pluto*

Which is the smallest planet?

Pluto is the smallest planet. Its diameter is 2200 kilometres. This is about two-thirds the size of our Moon.

Pluto   *The Moon*

What is the difference between a planet and a star?

A star is a huge ball of hot glowing gas, like the Sun. A planet is a world like the Earth. The Sun and stars produce their own light. The planets are lit by light from the Sun. In the night sky, you cannot tell the planets from the stars. They all look like tiny points of light, because they are far away. However, the planets are nearer than the stars. Through a powerful telescope, you can see that the planets are other worlds. The stars are so very distant that they still look like points of light, even through the most powerful telescope.

Where does the Solar System end?

The most distant planet, Pluto, is often thought to be at the edge of the Solar System. Its orbit takes it an average distance of 5900 million kilometres from the Sun. This is about a million times the width of the Atlantic Ocean between Europe and the United States. However, some comets are thought to travel halfway to the nearest star – a distance of about two light years. This would make the Solar System about four light years across, which is nearly 40 million million kilometres.

What is an orbit?

An orbit is the circular or oval path that something follows as it moves through space. The planets move in orbits around the Sun, and moons travel in orbits around planets. Satellites orbit the Earth. To get into orbit around the Earth, a spacecraft has to fly out into space beyond the atmosphere. It also has to accelerate to a speed of at least 28,200 kilometres per hour. This is equal to nearly 8 kilometres every second! If a spacecraft does not reach this speed, it will fall back to Earth.

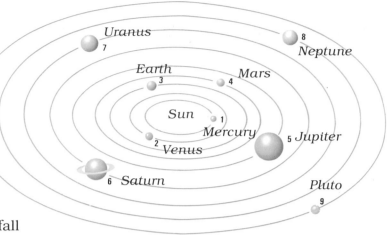

Saturn

Which planets have rings around them?

Three planets have rings around them – Jupiter, Saturn and Uranus. The rings are thin belts of rocks orbiting the planets. Saturn's rings make it the most beautiful planet in the sky. Astronomers believe that Neptune also has rings. We will know definitely when the space probe, Voyager 2, reaches Neptune in 1989.

Where are the inner and outer planets?

The inner planets are the four planets nearest to the Sun. They are Mercury, Venus, Earth and Mars. The five other planets – Jupiter, Saturn, Uranus, Neptune and Pluto – are much farther away from the Sun and are therefore called the outer planets.

Which planet is so hot that lead would melt there?

The hottest planet is not the planet nearest the Sun, which is Mercury. It is Venus, the second nearest. It is very hot on Venus because, unlike Mercury, it has an atmosphere. The atmosphere acts rather like the windows in a greenhouse, and helps to heat the surface of the planet. The temperature there is about 475°C, which is hot enough to melt several metals, including tin, lead and zinc.

Venus

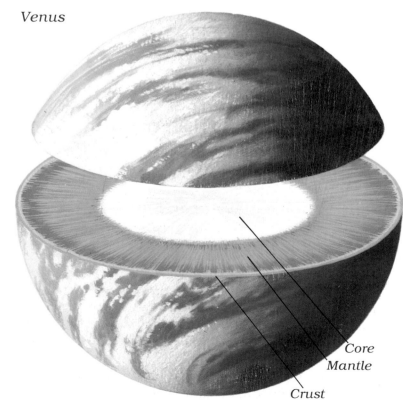

Core
Mantle
Crust

Which planet turns so slowly that one day lasts two years?

Mercury is so near the Sun that the Sun has slowed its rotation. It spins so slowly that one complete day on Mercury – from one sunrise to the next – takes 176 Earth days. This is equal to two of Mercury's years, which are 88 Earth days long. On Mercury, you would have two birthdays every day!

Mars

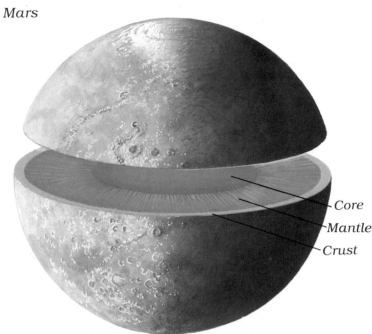

Core
Mantle
Crust

Mercury

Core
Mantle
Crust

What is the Red Planet?

The Red Planet is the fourth planet from the Sun – Mars. When it nears the Earth, it looks like a bright red star in the sky. Mars looks red because its surface is made of red soil and rock. Even its sky is red, because red dust floats in the thin atmosphere.

Which planet spins faster than any other?

The planet that spins the fastest is also the largest planet – Jupiter. It spins once around every 9 hours 50 minutes, $2\frac{1}{2}$ times as fast as the Earth. A point on Jupiter's equator is moving around the planet's centre at a speed of more than 45,000 kilometres per hour. This is so fast that it makes Jupiter bulge in the middle.

Does a planet have to be bigger than a moon?

A moon is always smaller than the planet around which it moves. A smaller body always orbits around a larger body, because the larger body has a greater force of gravity. However, not all moons are smaller than *all* planets. Our Moon and six other moons of the outer planets are all bigger than the planet Pluto. But Pluto may once have been a moon of Neptune. It escaped its parent planet long ago and became a planet itself.

Which planet could float on water?

If you could take the planets and place them in a vast ocean of water, then most of them would sink immediately. However, one would float. This planet is Saturn, which is the second largest planet in the Solar System. Because it is made mostly of gas and liquid, it is less dense or lighter than water and would float. All the other planets are more dense or heavier than water.

Do all planets and moons move in the same direction?

The Solar System is like a huge roundabout. All the planets move around the Sun in the same direction. If you were to look down from above the Sun's North Pole, you would see that all the planets circle the Sun in an anticlockwise direction. However, not all the moons obey this traffic rule. Most moons orbit their planets in an anticlockwise direction, but some go the other way. Jupiter has moons that go both ways. The moons will not crash into each other because they keep at different distances from Jupiter.

Are there any living things on other planets?

The Moon, and the planets and their moons, do not have air like our world. They are also very hot or very cold. We could not live there, neither could the animals and plants that live on Earth. Astronauts that went to the Moon did not find life there, nor did the Viking space probes that landed on Mars. It is very unlikely that there are any living things anywhere else in the Solar System.

No life could survive the heat on Mercury.

Are there any more planets beyond Pluto?

Astronomers believe that there may be an unknown planet beyond Pluto. They have searched for it with telescopes, but the mystery planet has not been found. If the planet does exist, it could disturb the paths of space probes moving among and beyond the outer planets. In this way, astronomers may discover the planet.

Meteors shoot across the night sky.

What is the difference between a meteor, a meteoroid, a meteorite and a shooting star?

A *shooting star* looks like a star that suddenly shoots across the night sky. It lasts only a second or two before disappearing. It is in fact not a star at all but a small particle of rock that strikes the Earth's atmosphere from space. It moves so fast that it heats up as it moves through the air, becoming white hot before burning away. A particle or piece of rock that moves through space is called a *meteoroid*. If it burns up in the atmosphere, it is called a shooting star or *meteor*. Some meteoroids are big enough to survive their fiery descent and strike the ground. These are called *meteorites*.

Where are meteorite craters to be seen?

Meteorites form craters when they strike the ground. There is a huge meteorite crater in Arizona in the United States. It is 1265 metres across, and was formed about 25,000 years ago. However, on Earth most meteorite craters become filled in and disappear. Elsewhere, they do not. The Moon, Mercury, Mars and its moons, and most of the moons of Jupiter are covered with meteorite craters.

The Barringer crater in Arizona

Do meteorites ever kill people?

As far as anyone knows, nobody has ever been killed by a falling meteorite. Meteorites are so few and far between that the chances of being hit by one are very, very low indeed.

What is a comet?

A comet is thought to be composed of small rocks and dust particles cemented together by frozen gas and ice. It orbits around the Sun and appears to hang in the sky like the Moon. However, although a comet does not seem to move fast, it is actually moving through space at about the same speed as a planet moves around the Sun.

Are comets dangerous?

We have little reason to fear comets. The Earth has even passed through the tail of Halley's comet with no ill effects.

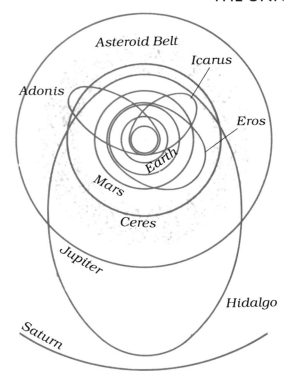

The orbits of five of the bigger asteroids: Ceres, Icarus, Eros, Adonis and Hidalgo.

Where are asteroids found?

Asteroids are small worlds that orbit the Sun as planets do. They are also called minor planets. The largest, Ceres, is about 1000 kilometres across. There are thousands of asteroids, most only a few kilometres across. They lie in a huge belt around the Sun between Mars and Jupiter.

The orbit of Halley's comet

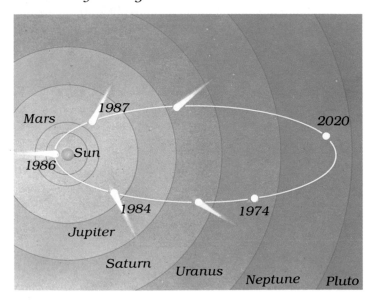

The Sun

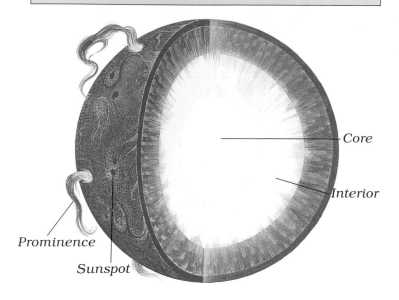

Core

Interior

Prominence

Sunspot

How big is the Sun?

The Sun is 1,392,500 kilometres across, 109 times the diameter of the Earth. It weighs 333,000 times as much as the Earth, and its volume is so huge that it could swallow·up 1,300,000 Earths. If the Earth were the size of a tennis ball, then the Sun would be as big as a house.

What is the Sun made of?

The Sun is a huge ball of hot gas. Its temperature is so high that it glows white hot, giving out light and heat rays. Most of the gas in the Sun is hydrogen. This is slowly turning into another gas, helium, inside the Sun. As it does so, it produces tremendous amounts of heat.

When did the Sun begin to shine?

The Sun began to shine about 5000 million years ago. It formed from a cloud of gas and dust floating in space. The cloud gradually got smaller and became thicker. As the cloud shrank, the centre heated up. Eventually, it became so hot that it began to glow and the Sun was born. The rest of the cloud formed the planets and everything else in the Solar System, including moons, asteroids and comets.

Does the Sun move?

The Sun appears to move across the sky from dawn to dusk. However, this motion is caused by the Earth spinning. The Sun only *seems* to be moving, and it is we who are moving and not the Sun. Nevertheless, the Sun moves in other ways. It spins like the Earth does, though much more slowly. Also, as the Earth moves around the Sun carrying the Moon with it, so the Sun moves around the centre of the Galaxy taking the Earth and the rest of the Solar System with it.

How hot is the Sun?

The temperature at the surface of the Sun is about 5500°C – hot enough to vaporize everything on Earth. The temperature at the centre of the Sun is far higher – about 15 million °C.

What happens during an eclipse of the Sun?

The Moon moves in front of the Sun during an eclipse of the Sun. It gets dim outside and the Sun appears to get smaller, like a new moon. In a total eclipse, the Sun disappears for a short time and it becomes dark and cold outside. During an eclipse of the Moon, the Moon seems to get smaller and may disappear. This is because the Earth moves in front of the Sun, and its shadow falls on the Moon.

Solar Eclipse

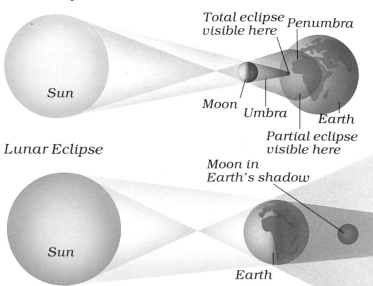

Total eclipse visible here · Penumbra

Sun

Moon · Umbra · Earth

Partial eclipse visible here

Lunar Eclipse

Moon in Earth's shadow

Sun

Earth

The Moon

How big is the Moon?

The Moon is 3476 kilometres across – about the same width as Australia. Its total area is less than four times the size of Europe.

The size of the Moon compared to the size of Australia

Where does the Moon come from?

The Moon formed when the Solar System was formed, at the same time as the Earth. This was about 4600 million years ago.

Why is the Moon covered in craters?

There are craters on Earth. They are made by meteorites crashing from space, and also by volcanoes. The same kinds of craters occur on the Moon. The action of the weather fills in or smooths out most of the craters on Earth. However, there is no weather on the Moon so the craters there remain unchanged.

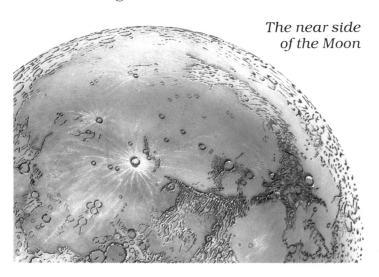

The near side of the Moon

How does the Moon stay up in the sky?

The Moon is pulled by the Earth's gravity, just like anything that falls to the ground. However, it does not crash to Earth because it is moving to one side too quickly. Instead, it 'falls' around the Earth in a path or orbit that is almost circular. In this way, it keeps about the same distance from the Earth. It is an average of 385,000 kilometres away, or 30 times the diameter of the Earth. If the Earth were a tennis ball, the Moon would be about the size of a marble 2 metres away.

Why does the shape of the Moon change in the sky?

Every four weeks, the Moon goes from a crescent-shaped new moon to a round full moon and back again. These changes are called phases. The Moon does not actually change shape. As it moves around the Earth, different parts become lit up by the Sun. We see only the lit-up parts.

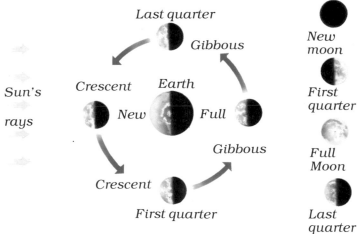

The phases of the Moon

How high could you jump on the Moon?

You could jump higher on the Moon than on Earth because your body would weigh six times less there. This is because the Moon's gravity is one-sixth of the gravity on Earth. However, this doesn't mean that you could jump six times as high as you can on Earth because you would have to wear a heavy and bulky spacesuit to stay alive.

Stars and Galaxies

Where do stars form?

Stars form in clouds of gas and dust, as the Sun did. Far away in space, there are huge clouds of gas and dust called nebulae. Some nebulae are luminous and shine with light, and it is there that stars are forming right now.

How far away is the nearest star?

The nearest star to the Earth is the Sun. It is 150 million kilometres away, or nearly 12,000 times the diameter of the Earth.

How far away is the most distant star?

Our Sun is one of about 100,000 million stars that make up the Galaxy. The most distant stars on the other side of the Galaxy to the Sun are about 80,000 light years away. However, there are millions of other galaxies much farther away, each containing millions of stars.

Which is the brightest star?

The brightest star in the sky is the Sun. It outshines all the other stars because it is so near to us. The brightest star in the *night* sky is Sirius. It actually produces 25 times as much light as the Sun. Other stars are even brighter, and may be as much as a million times more luminous than the Sun. But they all look fainter than Sirius because they are much farther away.

How many stars are there in the sky?

On a very clear night far from a town, you could count about 2000 stars in the sky. From all points on the Earth, about 6000 stars can be seen in all. With a telescope, many more fainter stars reveal themselves. There are millions upon millions of stars in the Universe.

Is the Sun an unusual kind of star?

To us on Earth, the Sun looks big and very bright. But this is only because we live close to the Sun. Compared with most stars, it is of average size and brightness and it is not in any way unusual.

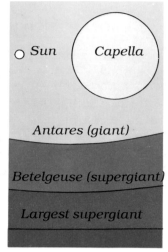

The Sun is much smaller than giant and supergiant stars.

What is a supernova?

A supernova is a star that suddenly flares up, becoming millions of times brighter. It gets so bright that it may be seen during the day, but it soon fades. A supernova is a very rare sight, because it is the explosion that marks the end of a large star.

Why do the stars twinkle?

The light from a star has to get through the atmosphere before it reaches our eyes. The atmosphere contains moving layers of air. The layers keep on bending the path of the starlight a little, and make the star appear to twinkle. In fact, the stars shine steadily.

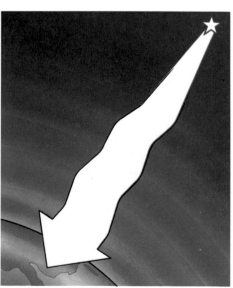

Stars only appear to twinkle.

What are constellations?

The stars form patterns in the night sky that never change. These patterns are called constellations. Long ago, people gave them names like The Swan, The Scorpion, The Plough and Orion The Hunter because the patterns resembled animals, familiar objects, people or gods. We still use their names for the constellations. Sometimes the names are in Latin. The Swan, for example, is Cygnus and The Scorpion is Scorpius.

Celestial sphere showing the constellations

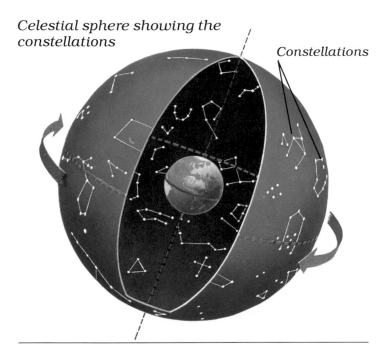

Constellations

What is the Milky Way?

The Milky Way is the name of the great band of stars that stretches across the night sky. When we look at the Milky Way, we are looking into the vast group of stars that make up our Galaxy.

What is a galaxy?

A galaxy is a great group of millions of stars. Our Galaxy, the Milky Way, is shaped like a flat disc with spiral arms of stars. It is about 100,000 light years across. There are millions of other galaxies in the Universe.

Two views of the Milky Way. The red arrows point to the position of the Sun.

Why can stars only be seen at night?

Stars cannot be seen during the day because the Sun is so bright. Its light spreads out over the sky, making it appear blue. The stars are still there in the sky, but our eyes adjust to the bright blue of the sky and cannot make out the fainter stars. At dawn and dusk, when the sunlight is pale, the brightest stars and planets can be seen.

What is a quasar?

Quasars are mysterious objects that astronomers discovered in 1960. They are sources of light or radio waves, like galaxies. However, they appear to be very far away, and the most distant objects known are quasars. Yet, they appear also to be very bright – as bright as hundreds of galaxies – but very much smaller than most galaxies. How could such a small body produce so much light? Possibly a black hole at the centre of the quasar makes it collapse in size and give out bright light before disappearing.

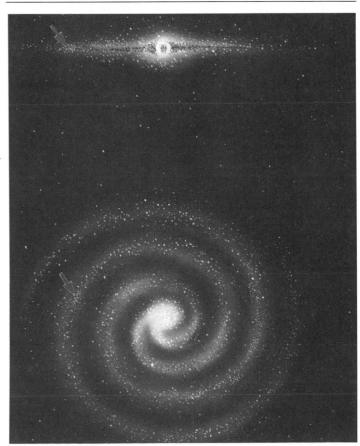

Space Exploration

Did the first astronomers have telescopes?

The ancient Greek astronomer Thales successfully predicted that an eclipse of the Sun would occur in 585 BC. This was more than 2000 years before the telescope was invented. Instead of telescopes, the ancient astronomers had instruments to measure how high the Sun, planets and stars were in the sky.

Who discovered that the Earth goes around the Sun?

As long ago as 260 BC, the Greek astronomer Aristarchus said that the Earth goes around the Sun. But most people could not believe that the Earth moves. It was not until 1728, almost 2000 years later, that he was proved right. Using a huge telescope, the British astronomer James Bradley saw that the stars appear to move very slightly as the Earth goes around the Sun.

Who discovered that the Earth is round?

From the way that a ship disappears over the horizon, people have long thought that the Earth must be round. It was not proved until the first ship sailed around the world in the 1500s. Long before, in about 240 BC, the Greek astronomer Eratosthenes worked out the correct circumference of the Earth. However, no one at that time could believe that the Earth was so big.

Who invented the telescope?

Hans Lippershey, a Dutch spectacle maker, invented the telescope in 1608. He, or an assistant, noted that things looked nearer when seen through two spectacle lenses. Lippershey mounted the lenses in a tube, thus making the first telescope. One year later, in 1609, the great Italian astronomer Galileo Galilei built a telescope and made several important discoveries.

Which was the first planet to be discovered?

The five nearest planets to us – Mercury, Venus, Mars, Jupiter and Saturn – have been known since prehistoric times. In 1781, the British astronomer Sir William Herschel accidentally discovered a new planet while searching the stars with his telescope. It was named Uranus. In fact, Uranus can be seen with the naked eye, but no one had realized that it was a planet.

Sir William Herschel's telescope

How did astronomers predict the discoveries of two planets?

In 1846, a British and a French astronomer said that an unknown planet was disturbing the orbit of the planet Uranus. Unknown to each other, they both worked out where the new planet would be seen in the sky. It was immediately discovered by a German astronomer exactly where the other astronomers had predicted it would be found. The new planet was called Neptune. Disturbances in its orbit eventually led to the discovery of another planet, Pluto, in 1930.

How big and powerful are astronomers' telescopes?

The biggest mirror telescope is in Hawaii. It has a 36-piece mirror 10 metres across. The biggest single-mirror telescopes are a 6-metre telescope in Russia and the 5-metre Hale telescope at Mount Palomar in the USA. The largest radio telescope, which gathers radio waves instead of light, is the Arecibo telescope in Puerto Rico. It has a dish 305 metres across. It too can detect objects at the edge of the Universe.

Who was the first man in space?

A Russian cosmonaut (astronaut) named Yuri Gagarin made the first manned spaceflight. He was launched into space aboard the spacecraft Vostok 1 on 12 April 1961, and made one orbit of the Earth before landing 1 hour 48 minutes later.

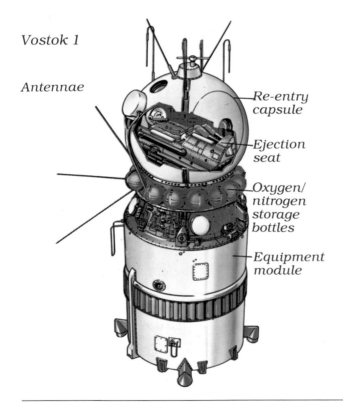

Vostok 1

Antennae

Re-entry capsule

Ejection seat

Oxygen/ nitrogen storage bottles

Equipment module

Who was the first woman in space?

The first woman to make a spaceflight was the Russian cosmonaut Valentina Tereshkova. She made a flight lasting three days aboard the spacecraft Vostok 6 in June 1963. During the flight, she completed 48 orbits of the Earth.

Who was the first person to step on the Moon?

The American astronaut Neil Armstrong became the first person to set foot on the Moon on 21 July 1969. As he descended from the lunar module of the Apollo 11 spacecraft and stepped on to the Moon, he said 'That's one small step for a man, one giant leap for mankind'. Armstrong was followed a little later by Edwin Aldrin.

Edwin Aldrin, the second man to step on the Moon

What is the most dangerous part of a spaceflight?

Astronauts face the most danger at the end of a spaceflight. When a spacecraft comes back from space, it is moving very fast indeed. As it enters the top layers of the atmosphere, the rush of air around the spacecraft begins to heat it up. The heating would be enough to make the spacecraft red-hot and kill the astronauts inside. To keep it cool and protect the astronauts, the spacecraft has a heatshield underneath. However, the spacecraft must enter the atmosphere with the heatshield facing forward, otherwise it will burn up.

When did the first spacecraft go into space?

The first rocket to go beyond the atmosphere into space was an American rocket fired aloft in 1949. But the first true spacecraft was the first satellite to go into orbit around the Earth. This was the Russian satellite Sputnik 1, which was launched into space on 4 October 1957. It had no person or animal aboard. Instead it contained machines that sent information back to Earth by radio.

How fast does a spacecraft travel?

To reach the Moon or any of the planets, a spacecraft has to be launched away from the Earth at a speed called escape velocity. This is 11 kilometres a second, or 40,000 kilometres an hour – fast enough to go once around the world in an hour. This speed is reached high above the Earth, and the spacecraft then coasts on through space to its destination. If it does not reach escape velocity, the spacecraft will either fall back to Earth or go into orbit around the Earth.

Have signals ever been received from space?

In 1931, an American radio engineer named Karl Jansky heard a strange radio noise. When he traced its origin, he discovered that it was coming from the stars. This is because stars and galaxies produce radio waves as well as light. In 1967, a British radio astronomer named Jocelyn Bell Burnell detected an on-off signal coming from space. It came from a kind of neutron star called a pulsar.

How big and powerful is the largest space rocket?

The most powerful rocket is the Energya booster first launched in Russia in 1987. It weighs 2500 tonnes and at lift-off its engines produce a thrust of 4000 tonnes. The American Saturn V rocket which launched Apollo astronauts to the Moon from 1969 to 1972 was 111 metres high (20 times as high as a two-storey house) with the thrust of forty jumbo jets!

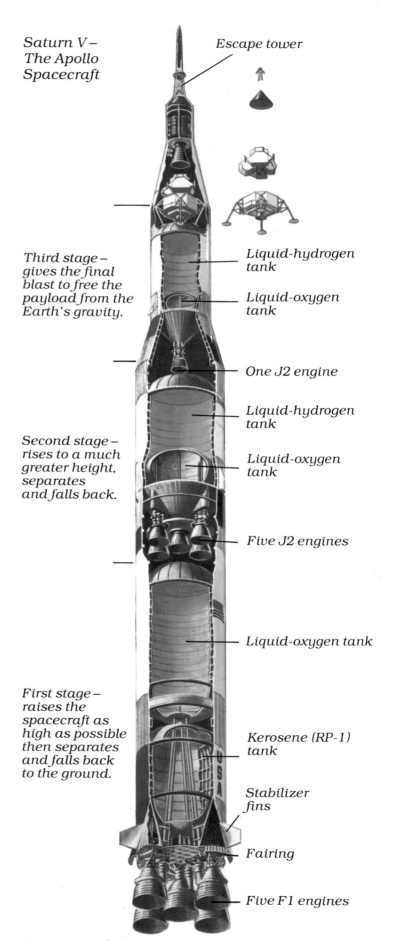

Saturn V – The Apollo Spacecraft

Escape tower

Third stage – gives the final blast to free the payload from the Earth's gravity.

Liquid-hydrogen tank

Liquid-oxygen tank

One J2 engine

Liquid-hydrogen tank

Second stage – rises to a much greater height, separates and falls back.

Liquid-oxygen tank

Five J2 engines

Liquid-oxygen tank

First stage – raises the spacecraft as high as possible then separates and falls back to the ground.

Kerosene (RP-1) tank

Stabilizer fins

Fairing

Five F1 engines

What do satellites do?

A satellite is any body or object that moves around another. The Moon is a satellite of the Earth, and the Earth and other planets are satellites of the Sun. However, most people use the word satellite to mean a man-made object that orbits the Earth. These satellites make scientific observations of space and of the Earth below, sending back pictures that help us to forecast the weather, for example. Satellites also send television programmes and telephone calls from one continent to another.

Will people ever go to the planets and stars?

There are no spacecraft powerful enough to send people to the planets. To build such spacecraft and send them would cost a huge amount of money. Also, space probes can explore the planets for us. The stars are so far away that it would take a spacecraft travelling at its fastest about 20,000 years to reach the nearest star. It seems unlikely that people will ever go there.

Where do space probes go?

A space probe is an unmanned spacecraft that flies to the Moon or planets. It may land on the Moon or planets, go into orbit around them, or fly past them. The space probe contains cameras and other equipment to send pictures and information back to Earth by radio.

The space probe Voyager 2 flew past four planets and out of the solar system.

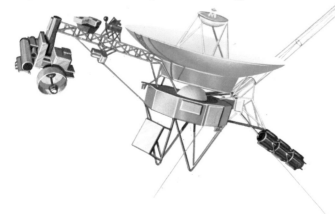

The space shuttle blasts off on the back of its huge fuel tank.

What does a space shuttle do?

The space shuttle is a very versatile spacecraft. Unlike all earlier spacecraft, it can be used again and again. It takes off from Earth like a rocket, but lands like an aircraft. The space shuttle cannot fly to the Moon or planets. It goes into orbit around the Earth. There, the crew can do scientific work, place satellites in orbit, and visit satellites and space stations in orbit.

How much would you weigh in space?

If you were to travel in space, you would weigh nothing at all for most of your flight! Only when the engines were firing at the beginning and end of the flight would you have any weight. In between, you would float in mid-air in the cabin of your spacecraft. This is because gravity cannot pull the astronaut to the floor of the cabin.

How can people live in space?

There is nothing in space to keep people alive – no air, no water and no food. Without protection, a person would die in seconds. A spacecraft provides air, water and food for astronauts. Outside, they must wear spacesuits. These have an air or oxygen supply, and food and water if necessary. The spacesuit also has cooling or heating systems, for it can be very hot or very cold in space depending on whether the astronaut is in sunshine or not.

THE EARTH

When did the Earth form?

The Earth formed about 4600 million years ago. It formed in the cloud of gas and dust that condensed to make the Sun and all the planets. Grains of rock came together in the cloud, eventually forming a globe of rock. The rock was red-hot and liquid at first, and cooled and hardened later.

Why is the world round?

The world is round for the same reason that a raindrop and a bubble are round. If possible, a liquid naturally shapes itself into a ball. This happens if the liquid is falling through the air, like a raindrop, or floating like a bubble. When the Earth formed, it was hot and liquid. Because it was floating in space, it became round. When the liquid rock cooled and hardened into solid rock, the Earth stayed round.

How big is the Earth?

The Earth's circumference (the distance around the world) at the equator is 40,076 kilometres. Its diameter (the distance across the Earth) at the equator is 12,757 kilometres. The Earth is slightly smaller when measured between the Poles. If you could put the world on a pair of scales, it would weigh nearly 6000 million million million tonnes. However, the Earth is getting several thousand tonnes heavier each year, because of the meteoroids that strike it.

The formation of the Earth

What is it like inside the Earth?

The Earth is a huge ball of rock. If you could tunnel down to the centre, you would go through several layers. The first layer is the crust of the Earth. It is as little as 6 kilometres thick beneath the oceans. Then comes a thick layer of rock called the mantle, which goes almost halfway down to the Earth's centre. As it gets deeper, it gets hotter and beneath the mantle is a layer of hot, liquid rock called the outer core. Finally, at the centre of the Earth is the inner core – a huge ball of hot but solid rock. It begins 5000 kilometres beneath our feet. At the centre, the temperature is thought to reach 4500°C.

How much land is there?

On the Earth, land covers nearly 150 million square kilometres. This is equal to about 30,000 square metres of land for every person on Earth. The land covers only 29% of the Earth's surface. The remaining 71% of the Earth's surface is covered by the oceans and seas.

The Earth: facts

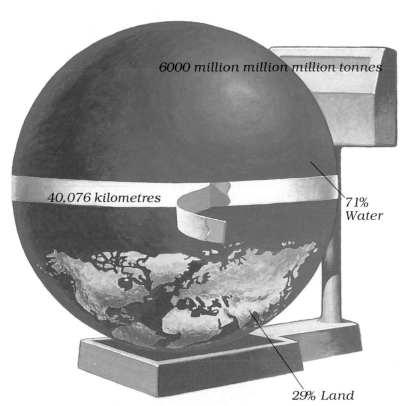

6000 million million million tonnes

40,076 kilometres

71% Water

29% Land

Planet Earth

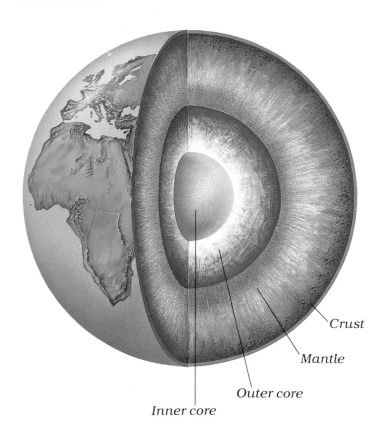

Crust

Mantle

Outer core

Inner core

Who made the first map of the world?

People made maps of the world long ago, but they were nothing like the maps we have today. They did not know that continents such as North and South America, and Antarctica, exist. Their maps showed only part of the world. The first maps that look anything like the world we know today were drawn in the 1500s, when people had begun to sail around the world. One of the best was made by Mercator, a Flemish mapmaker, who developed the use of map projection in 1568.

What are latitude and longitude?

Latitude and longitude are the lines marked on a map or globe of the world. The lines that go from north to south are the lines of longitude. Lines of latitude go from east to west. Navigators work out the position of their ship or aircraft in latitude and longitude. The position is where the lines of latitude and longitude cross.

The Atmosphere

What is air made of?

Air is made of invisible gases. The main gas is nitrogen, and then come oxygen and argon. There is also some water vapour in the air unless it is very dry.

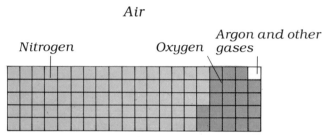

Air

Nitrogen   Oxygen   Argon and other gases

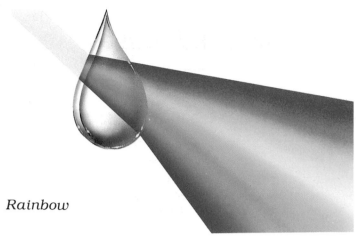

Rainbow

How many colours are there in a rainbow?

On the inside of a rainbow is a layer of violet light, and then come indigo, blue, green, yellow, orange and finally red on top of the rainbow. This makes seven colours, though you may not see them all, particularly indigo.

How much does air weigh?

There is about 160 kilometres of air above your head. Although air may seem to have no weight, all this air presses down on the ground just like any solid object. Its weight on every square metre of the ground is about 10 tonnes.

Where does a rainbow end?

Rainbows form in falling rain and in clouds of spray when sunlight falls on them. So, the rainbow is as far away from you as the rain or spray is, and it ends (and begins) in the rain or spray. To see a rainbow, the Sun must be behind you.

Why is the sky blue?

During the day, light from the Sun travels through the air to reach our eyes. However, not all the light rays move in a straight line. The white light of the Sun in fact consists of a mixture of colours – the colours of the rainbow. The blue rays are scattered by the air, and come to our eyes from all angles in the sky. This makes the sky look blue.

What is a mirage?

On a hot day, you can often see what appear to be pools of water lying in the road. However, as you get nearer to them, the pools disappear and there is nothing to be seen. You have been tricked by a mirage. The layers of warm air above the road act like a mirror. What you see is a reflection of the sky. As you get near, the reflection disappears.

Why is the sky red at sunset?

The sky looks blue during the day because the air scatters the blue rays in the Sun's light. At sunset, the Sun is low in the sky and the Sun's light travels through more air than during the day. The extra air scatters all the other colours in the light except red. Only the red rays come straight to the eye, and so the Sun looks red.

Where can you see the Northern Lights and Southern Lights?

You can see the Northern Lights in or near the Arctic, and the Southern Lights in or near the Antarctic. They are marvellous displays of coloured lights that appear in huge patterns in the night sky. They are caused by electrical particles from the Sun hitting the Earth's atmosphere.

Time and Seasons

Why do we have seasons every year?

In most parts of the world, there are four seasons every year. The seasons happen because the Earth tilts as it goes around the Sun. In places where it is summer, the Earth is tilted towards the Sun and it is warm. In winter, the Earth is tilted away from the Sun and it is cold. However, in the tropics the tilt is very small and seasons do not occur. It is hot all the year round.

Where does one day suddenly change into another?

There are places in the world where it suddenly becomes tomorrow or yesterday if you cross an imaginary line. This line is drawn on maps and is called the International Date Line. It runs through the Pacific Ocean from north to south. On the eastern side of the line, the time is always 24 hours behind the time on the western side. When you cross the line in an aircraft or aboard ship, you immediately gain or lose a day.

This diagram shows how seasons change as the Earth moves around the Sun.

What is equal about an equinox and unequal about a solstice?

The answer is night and day. Equinoxes and solstices are certain days of the year. Equinox means 'equal night', and it is the date during the spring and autumn when the day and night last exactly the same time – twelve hours each. The spring equinox is on or near 21 March, and the autumnal equinox is on or near 22 September. Solstices are the dates during the summer or winter when the day or night is longest and the night or day shortest.

Can the same day be both the longest and shortest day of the year?

On or near 21 June, the longest day and the shortest night occur in the northern hemisphere. However, on the very same day, it is the shortest day and the longest night in the southern hemisphere. This is because it is midsummer in the northern hemisphere and midwinter in the southern hemisphere. The same thing happens again on or near 22 December, but the other way around. These dates are called the summer solstice or winter solstice, depending on the season of the year. If you went to the equator, midway between the two hemispheres, you would find that every day has twelve hours of daylight and twelve hours of night. Every day would be the longest – and shortest – of the year!

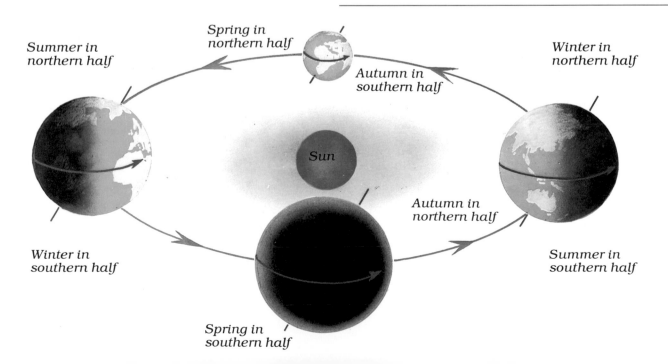

Summer in northern half

Spring in northern half

Winter in northern half

Autumn in southern half

Sun

Autumn in northern half

Winter in southern half

Spring in southern half

Summer in southern half

Weather and Climate

Why does rain fall from the sky?

Rain falls from the sky because there is water in the air. The water is in the form of water vapour, which is invisible like a gas. High in the sky, it is cold and the water vapour condenses to form tiny droplets of water. These droplets gather to produce clouds, and then the droplets flow together to make bigger drops of water. When the drops become too big and heavy to stay in the clouds, they fall as rain.

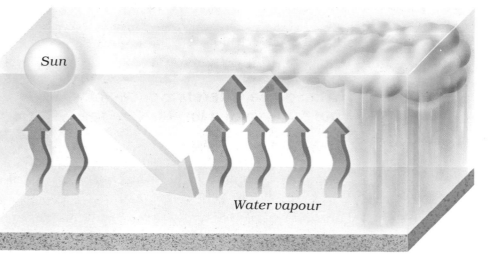

Sun

Water vapour

How is rainfall measured?

An instrument called a rain gauge is placed outside in the rain to measure how much rain falls. The depth of water that collects in the rain gauge is measured to find the rainfall, and it is measured in millimetres.

Why is it dry in deserts?

Deserts are found around the world on both sides of the tropics. It is very dry in these regions because the winds mostly blow away from them. The winds do not bring in any damp air to cause rain. In the Atacama Desert in Chile, it did not rain for about 400 years up to 1971.

Why do winds blow?

The heat of the Sun makes the air move and causes winds to blow. Winds blow in huge patterns over the Earth's surface. In the tropics, the Sun heats the air. The heat makes the air lighter, and it rises. Air then moves towards the tropics to make up for the rising air, so that winds blow towards the tropics. These air movements cause other air movements, setting up patterns of winds around the world.

Snowflake

The Sun heats the Earth's surface causing hot air and water vapour to rise into the air. This water vapour becomes rain.

Rain gauge

How do snow and hail form in the sky?

Both snow and hail are frozen rain. If it is cold enough, the tiny water droplets in a cloud will freeze and form ice crystals that gather into snowflakes. If raindrops freeze, hailstones form. Snow may form in clouds in summer. But it melts before reaching the ground and falls as rain. Hailstones are thicker and do not melt. Hail may therefore fall in summer, especially in thunderstorms. The hailstones may weigh as much as a kilogram, and can cause severe damage.

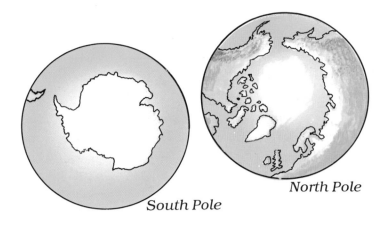

South Pole

North Pole

Which is colder – the North Pole or the South Pole?

It gets colder at the South Pole than it ever gets at the North Pole. The lowest temperature ever recorded was at Vostock, Antarctica, not far from the South Pole. It fell to $-89.2°C$ on 21 July 1983.

Where does frost come from?

The white layer of frost that covers the ground on cold mornings comes out of the air. The air contains invisible water vapour which freezes where it meets the cold ground, forming a thin layer of ice crystals. This is frost.

What happens in a monsoon?

It rains – very heavily. The monsoon is the name of the rainy season in India and other warm countries. As the summer arrives, a storm breaks and it suddenly begins to rain. The wet season lasts until the autumn, and then it becomes dry. It stays dry until the monsoon comes again the next year. This kind of weather is caused by winds that are also called monsoons.

Why does lightning strike?

A flash of lightning is a huge spark of electricity. During a thunderstorm, electric charges of millions of volts build up in the clouds. Electric charges build up on the ground too. When the charges become powerful enough, electricity runs through the air between them, causing a flash of lightning. The lightning strikes between a cloud and the ground, or between two clouds.

What is sheet lightning?

Sheet lightning does not look like the zigzag flashes of lightning that you normally see. It produces a sudden glow of light in the sky. In fact, it is no different from ordinary lightning. Sheet lightning is simply ordinary lightning seen through clouds in the sky.

How far away is thunder and lightning?

A flash of lightning causes a thunderclap. Light from the flash travels almost instantly to your eyes. The sound of the thunderclap travels more slowly, and arrives a few seconds later. If you count the seconds between the flash and the thunder, you can work out the distance of the flash of lightning. Every three seconds is equal to one kilometre.

What is the difference between a hurricane and a tornado?

Hurricanes are huge and violent storms. They form out at sea in tropical parts of the Pacific, North Atlantic and Indian Oceans, and may then blow inland. In a hurricane, the wind may reach 300 kilometres an hour, causing great destruction and flooding. Tornadoes are twisting columns of air even more violent than hurricanes. However, they cause damage only along a narrow path. They usually strike in the United States, southern Russia and Australia.

Lightning flashes in a stormy sky.

The Oceans

How deep is the ocean?

The deepest ocean is the Pacific Ocean. In the Marianas Trench near the Philippines, the ocean bed descends to a record depth of 11,033 metres.

How many oceans are there?

There are four oceans. The biggest is the Pacific Ocean, which is almost as big as all the other oceans put together. Then come the Atlantic Ocean, Indian Ocean and Arctic Ocean. The southern part of the Pacific, Atlantic and Indian Oceans, which surrounds Antarctica, is sometimes known as the Antarctic Ocean or Southern Ocean. So you could say that there are five oceans.

Where would you find the continental shelf?

Every time you walk down a beach and into the sea, you are walking on to the continental shelf. The shelf is a huge ledge of rock that lies under the sea around the coast of a continent. It slopes gently away beneath the sea, reaching a depth of 120 to 360 metres. Then the sea bed falls steeply away, rather like an underwater cliff, down to the ocean floor.

Continental shelf

Why do waves move on the sea?

Waves move through the water because the wind blows them. In a strong wind, the waves are high. Although the waves move, the water does not (except where the wave breaks at the shore). The water only goes up and down, as you can see when a wave passes a boat. The wind makes the water move up and down in such a way that a wave appears on the surface.

Why is the sea salty?

The sea is salty because sea water has salt dissolved in it. Most of the salt is the same as the table salt you put on food. The salt comes from rivers that flow into the sea. The rivers dissolve a little salt from rocks over which they flow, and the dissolved salt gathers in the sea.

Why do tides rise and fall?

The Moon causes the tides. The Moon's pull of gravity is strong enough to raise the level of the water in the ocean, though not by more than about half a metre. The rise in level occurs on the side of the Earth nearest the Moon. The motion of the Earth through space causes another similar rise to occur on the other side of the Earth. As the Earth spins once in a day, the sea moves under these two rises in level. Two high tides occur every day as the sea level rises. In between the level falls, and there are two low tides.

What is a tidal wave?

A tidal wave occurs when an earthquake shakes the ocean floor. This action generates a wave throughout the depth of the ocean, and it is therefore far more powerful than the normal surface waves. The wave is not high in mid-ocean, but it moves very quickly – up to 800 kilometres an hour. As it reaches the coast, the water piles up into a huge wave. It roars ashore, destroying any towns that lie in its path. Tidal wave is not a good name for this kind of wave, as it has nothing to do with tides. It should be called a *tsunami*, a Japanese word meaning giant wave.

Where do whirlpools occur?

Whirlpools occur where one current of water meets another. As the two currents come together, the water swirls around in a whirlpool. Rocks, tides and strong winds may also cause currents to form whirlpools. A whirlpool is also called a maelstrom, from the name of a current that flows through the Lofoten Islands off the coast of Norway. The Maelstrom produces whirlpools powerful enough to suck down boats.

What is a fjord?

A fjord or fiord is an inlet of the sea that is surrounded by mountains or hills. The water in a fjord is often very deep – as much as 1000 metres or more. Fjords were formed long ago when glaciers carved out deep valleys, and the valleys later became filled by the sea.

Iceberg

Fjord

How big are icebergs?

Icebergs are much bigger than they look. You can only see about one tenth of the whole iceberg above water; eight to nine times as much ice is hidden below the water. The largest icebergs are found in the Antarctic Ocean, near the South Pole. They are about 100 metres high above water, but may be more than 300 kilometres long.

What is the difference between an ocean, a sea, a gulf and a bay?

These four stretches of water are different in size and location. The largest bodies of water are the oceans. At the edges of the oceans, there are smaller stretches of salt water called seas. For example, the North Sea is on one side of the Atlantic Ocean. Other seas, such as the Mediterranean Sea and Dead Sea, are almost completely surrounded by land. Gulfs and bays are bodies of water that penetrate into the land, gulfs being larger than bays.

Rivers and Lakes

Where is the longest river?

The longest river in the world is in Africa. It is the River Nile, and it is 6670 kilometres long.

Why do some rivers have deltas?

Sometimes a large river does not flow straight into the sea, but divides into several small rivers or channels instead. A delta forms because the river water deposits mud through which the smaller rivers or channels carve their way to reach the sea. A delta is named after the Greek letter Δ (delta) because of its triangular shape.

Where are the largest and deepest lakes?

Both of them are in Russia. The largest lake is the Caspian Sea at the border of Iran. It is not really a sea because it is totally surrounded by land. It is called a sea only because it is so big. In area, it extends 360,700 square kilometres – nearly twice the size of the United Kingdom. The deepest lake in the world, Lake Baikal, is in Siberia in eastern Russia. Its greatest depth is 1940 metres.

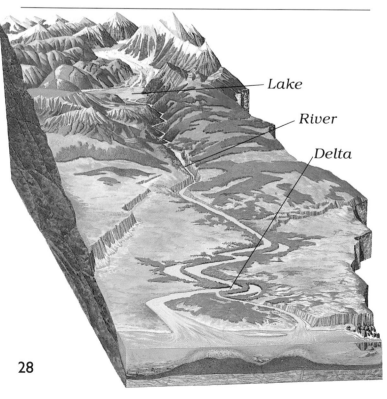

Lake

River

Delta

Do rivers and lakes last for ever?

No. Rivers and lakes may have long lifetimes of many thousands of years, but they eventually come to an end. As a river flows over the land, the water wears away the rock beneath. Very slowly, the river levels out the land until it is flat, and then it ceases to flow. Rivers also dry up if they are not fed with water. Lakes are fed by rivers carrying particles of soil. Gradually, the particles fill up the lake. So do the remains of dead water plants. The lake shrinks, and the water becomes a marsh. Then trees grow and it turns into dry land.

What is an estuary?

An estuary is the final part of a river, where it opens out and meets the sea. It is also called the mouth of the river. Tides may rise and fall in the estuary, exposing large banks of mud through which the river winds its way to the sea.

How high is the highest waterfall?

The highest waterfall is Angel Falls in Venezuela.

The water falls 807 metres in a single drop, and the whole waterfall is 979 metres high.

Angel Falls, Venezuela

How fast do waterfalls move?

Slowly, a whole waterfall moves upriver because the rapid flow of water wears away the rock ledge over which it falls. Niagara Falls, at the border of the United States and Canada, is moving at the rate of a metre every year.

Caves

Waves carve out caves on both sides of a headland.

The caves meet, forming a natural arch with a blow-hole in the surface.

What makes caves?

The action of waves beating away at the rock day after day carves out caves in cliffs by the sea. Underground caverns form in limestone, because underground streams flow through the rock and slowly dissolve away the limestone.

How deep can caves be?

The deepest caves in the world, which are in France, go down more than a kilometre below the ground.

Where would you find an ice cave?

Caves made of ice occur in glaciers. At the bottom of a glacier, where the ice melts, caves often form. The cave glows with deep blue light that comes through the ice from outside.

What is the difference between a stalactite and a stalagmite?

Stalactites and stalagmites are the beautiful stone columns that form in caves. Stalactites hang down from the roof of a cavern. Stalagmites grow up from the floor. They form as water drips through the roof. The drips leave tiny deposits of mineral behind, causing a stalactite to grow down. Where the drips strike the cave floor, a stalagmite grows up. Eventually, the two may meet and form a pillar.

How fast do stalactites and stalagmites grow?

Most stalactites and stalagmites grow very slowly indeed. It may take them as long as 2000 years to grow only one centimetre. However, some are much faster, and may grow this much in as little as a year or so.

A section through limestone shows numerous caves and tunnels.

1. Stalagmites
2. Stalactites
3. Natural columns
4. Stream entering from surface of rock
5. Stream re-emerging at base of limestone

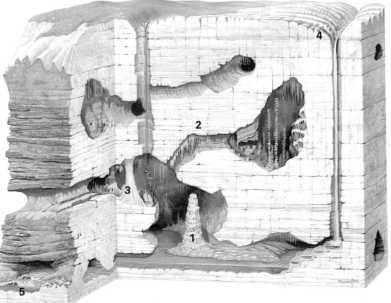

Mountains, Volcanoes and Earthquakes

Snowy peaks

Where is the highest mountain?

The highest mountain known is not Mount Everest – nor is it on Earth! It is Olympus Mons (Mount Olympus) on Mars, and it is about 29,000 metres high – over three times as high as Mount Everest. Mount Everest, which is on the border of Nepal and Tibet, is 8848 metres high.

How do mountains and valleys form?

Forces within the Earth push up the land to create mountains – and to form valleys between the mountains. Sections of the Earth's crust called plates slowly collide with each other. The impact makes the crust buckle and fold where the plates meet, producing mountains and valleys. The action is very slow, taking millions of years. Valleys also form slowly as rivers and glaciers wear away rock. Volcanoes, on the other hand, form quickly. A volcano grows as lava (liquid rock) pours from the ground and sets hard to give solid rock.

Why are high mountains covered in snow?

The tops of high mountains have snow on them because the air is very cold there. It gets colder the higher you go up a mountain. About every 1000 metres in height, the temperature falls by 5°C. Some mountains have snow on them in summer – they are so high that it is always freezing on top.

How fast do glaciers move?

Glaciers are rivers made of ice. They move down a mountainside and over the land just as rivers do, but much more slowly. Most glaciers move only a metre or so every day, and many are even slower. The glacier ends where it gets so warm that the ice melts, or it reaches the sea.

Are high mountains older or younger than low mountains?

Ranges of high mountains are younger than ranges of low mountains. The reason for this is that low mountain ranges were once higher, and have been worn down over many millions of years. High mountain ranges formed more recently, and have not yet worn down.

What sets off an avalanche?

An avalanche is a sudden fall of snow and ice down a mountainside. Avalanches are very dangerous because they can bury and kill people. They happen when so much snow falls that the layers of snow on the mountainside become too heavy and suddenly give way and slide or fall down. Avalanches also happen in spring when the warm weather begins to melt the snow so that it slides more easily. Earthquakes, and even sudden loud sounds, can also cause avalanches.

What makes a volcano erupt?

When a volcano erupts, red-hot lava (liquid rock) flows from the top and smoke and ashes pour into the sky. Inside the volcano, a pipe leads down far underground, where it is very hot. The lava is forced up the pipe from chambers of liquid rock deep below. Usually, the eruption soon stops and the pipe is blocked. Years later, the volcano may erupt again as the lava forces its way back up the volcano. It can cause so much pressure to build up that the volcano suddenly explodes, often without warning.

Why do some countries have volcanoes and earthquakes?

There are about 500 volcanoes in the world, and they occur only in certain parts of the world. Earthquakes shake the ground in these places too. These places are at the edges of huge plates or sections in the Earth's crust. The plates slowly move past or towards each other. The movements set off earthquakes and volcanic eruptions in the countries above the edges of the plates.

What happens in an earthquake?

In an earthquake, the ground suddenly begins to shake. The shaking lasts for a few seconds or minutes, and may be strong enough to make buildings fall down. Earthquakes happen where there are great cracks in the rocks below ground. The rocks on each side of the crack suddenly slide past each other. This makes the ground shake.

Which volcano caused the most destruction?

The most disastrous volcanic eruption in memory is that of Krakatoa in Indonesia. It exploded in 1883, killing more than 36,000 people. Most died from the tsunami (tidal wave) caused by the explosion. It was 36 metres high. The explosion was heard about 5000 kilometres away! However, a volcanic explosion five times more powerful occurred in Greece in about 1645 BC. The remains of this volcano may be seen on the island of Santorini or Thera. No one knows how much destruction it caused, but it probably gave rise to the legend of Atlantis.

Where do the worst earthquakes happen?

The worst earthquakes have happened in China. In 1556, an earthquake at Shensi killed over 800,000 people, the most disastrous ever known. Then in 1976, history repeated itself. An earthquake at Tangshan killed 750,000 people. In these two earthquakes, as many people as live in Northern Ireland, Nebraska or South Australia died.

A section cut through a volcanic region

1. *Underground chamber*
2. *Central vent*
3. *Side vent*
4. *Ash*
5. *Lava*
6. *Alternate layers of ash and lava*

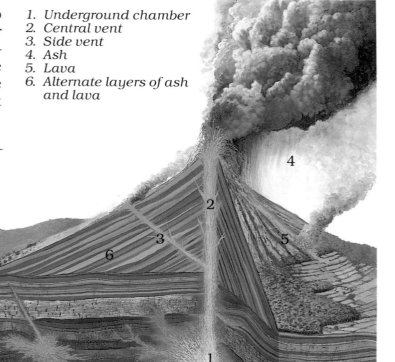

Natural Resources

What is the difference between a rock, a stone, an ore and a mineral?

Rock is the hard material that is found in the ground. Stone is another name for rock, and a large piece is called a rock or boulder and a small piece a stone or pebble. Rock and stone are made of substances called minerals. Limestone is a rock made of the mineral calcite or calcium carbonate. Many rocks contain several minerals. An ore is a rock that contains useful minerals. Metals are made from the minerals in ores.

How many kinds of rocks are there?

There are three main kinds of rocks, depending on how they formed. *Sedimentary* rocks formed long ago in layers, often at the bottom of the sea. They include limestone, conglomerate and sandstone. *Igneous* rocks formed from liquid rock like the lava in volcanoes, which cooled and became solid. They include granite, obsidian and basalt. *Metamorphic* rocks formed from sedimentary rocks or igneous rocks that were changed by the action of heat or by some other cause. They include marble and slate.

How old are rocks?

The oldest rocks known are about 4600 million years old, which is the same age as the Earth itself. These rocks are found in meteorites from space and on the Moon. On Earth, rocks formed later and so they are not so old.

In what way are marble, chalk and limestone alike?

Marble, chalk and limestone look very different from each other. Marble is a hard white rock with streaks of colour in it. It is used to make fine buildings and statues. Chalk is a soft white stone that you can use to write. Limestone is light grey stone used to make roads and cement. Yet all these kinds of rocks and stones are made of the same mineral – calcium carbonate. They look different because they formed in different ways.

Which rock is so light that it floats in water?

Pumice is a rock that is so light that it floats. This is because it is not completely solid, but has bubbles of air inside. The bubbles got into the rock because pumice formed from the lava (liquid rock) that pours from volcanoes. The lava may froth with bubbles and then set hard, giving pumice.

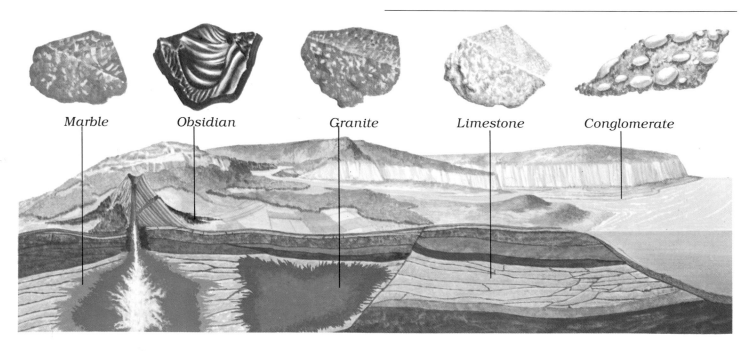

Marble   *Obsidian*   *Granite*   *Limestone*   *Conglomerate*

Why are gems valuable?

Gems are precious stones, such as diamonds and emeralds. They are found in rocks in the ground. The stones have lovely colours, and can be cut in special ways to make them shine with light. Gem stones are valuable because they can be made to look so attractive, and also because they are rare.

Sapphire *Diamond* *Emerald*

Where does salt come from?

The table salt you put on food comes from the mineral called salt. Its chemical name is sodium chloride. Salt occurs in sea water, in which it is dissolved, and as a solid mineral underground. The salt is obtained by allowing shallow pools of sea water to evaporate in the Sun, and salt is left behind. Salt is also mined underground.

Why does coal catch fire?

Coal is hard, like a rock, and yet it burns, which no rocks do. The reason is that coal is not made of rock or stone, but of wood – and wood can burn. Coal is a special kind of wood, of course. It is the remains of trees that lived millions of years ago. After they died the trees were buried, and under the ground, they gradually changed into coal.

Where is oil found?

Oil lies under the ground in many countries, and under the sea offshore. Oil is made of the remains of plants and animals that lived millions of years ago. Deposits of oil formed underground where the remains were buried and then trapped in the rocks that formed around them. Oil is the most important fuel in the world. The countries that produce the most oil are Russia, the United States, Saudi Arabia and Mexico.

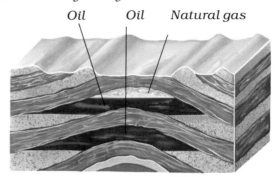

Beneath the surface of the Earth

Oil   Oil   Natural gas

What is natural about natural gas?

Natural gas comes from below the ground, like oil. It formed in the same way as oil. It is called natural gas because it formed in a natural way. The other kinds of gases that we burn in cookers and heaters are made at gas works.

An offshore oil rig

Places Around the World

How many continents are there?

A continent is a huge mass of land surrounded by water. The Earth has at least five continents: Africa, America, Antarctica, Australia and Eurasia. Strictly speaking, Africa and Eurasia are in fact joined together at Sinai in Egypt, but they are always counted as two continents. North America and South America are also usually thought of as two continents, and so are Europe and Asia – making a possible seven continents in all. The biggest continent is Asia, which is just bigger than North and South America put together. Its area is 42,700,000 square kilometres.

Do continents move?

The continents are not still, but are moving away or towards each other at speeds of about 2 centimetres a year. Although this is very slow, it is fast enough to change the map of the world over millions of years.

Where do two continents almost touch?

Continents almost touch each other at several places in the world. Asia and America are only 90 kilometres apart at the Bering Strait between the Pacific and Arctic Oceans. Europe and Africa come within 13 kilometres of each other at the Strait of Gibraltar, and Europe and Asia are separated by less than a kilometre at the Bosporus in Turkey. These last two continents are in fact joined by a bridge there.

Where is the equator?

The equator is a line that runs from east to west around the centre of the world. It is marked as 0° latitude on maps and globes, and divides the northern hemisphere from the southern hemisphere. There is no actual line on the ground. The largest countries through which the equator passes are Colombia, Brazil, Zaire, Kenya and Indonesia.

Six of the seven continents are on the map. Antarctica is at the South Pole.

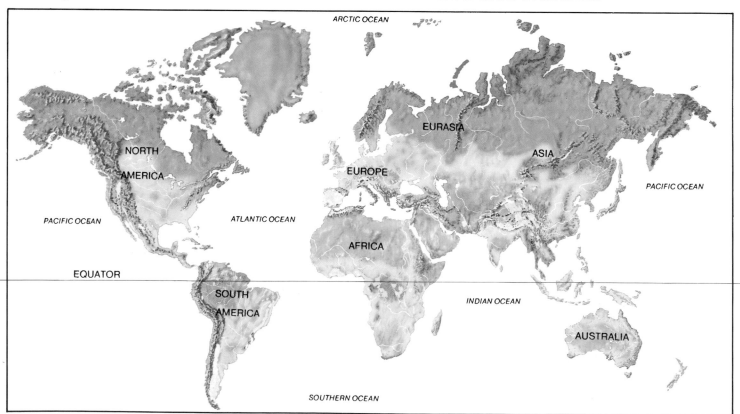

34

The Grand Canyon, Arizona

Where are the Tropics?

The Tropics are the regions of the world that are on or near the equator. It is always very warm in the Tropics, because they are the regions that are nearest the Sun.

A beach in the Tropics

Where is the Grand Canyon?

The Grand Canyon is in Arizona in the United States. It is as much as 29 kilometres wide and 1700 metres deep in places. Furthermore, it is the longest gorge in the world, being 349 kilometres in length. The Grand Canyon was formed by the Colorado River cutting deep into the rock.

Is Greenland really green?

Most of Greenland looks white, and is far from green. This is because Greenland lies mainly in the Arctic, and is mostly covered by ice and snow. Only the coast is green. Greenland got its odd name because when European explorers reached it, their first sight was of green grass.

What is the difference between the Arctic and Antarctic?

The Arctic is the region of the world around the North Pole. The Antarctic is the region around the South Pole. Both regions are very cold. The Arctic consists of an ice-covered ocean, the Arctic Ocean, surrounded mainly by land. The Antarctic consists of an ice-covered continent, Antarctica, surrounded by ocean.

Where is the Dead Sea?

The Dead Sea lies between Israel and Jordan. The surface is 392 metres below sea level, the lowest place on Earth. The Dead Sea is not really a sea but a large lake, because it is surrounded by land. The water is so salty that you cannot sink in it. But it is also so salty that no fish can live in the water, and this is why it is called the Dead Sea.

Where is Death Valley?

Death Valley is a deep valley in California in the United States. It is 86 metres below sea level, the lowest point in the western hemisphere. The valley is a desert, and is the hottest place in North America. It got its name in 1849 when pioneers nearly died trying to cross it.

Death Valley, California

Where is 'The Land of Fire'?

In 1520, the explorer Ferdinand Magellan was approaching the southern tip of South America on the first voyage around the world. As he passed the islands near the Cape, he saw many fires on the shore. They were not volcanoes, but were bonfires lit by the people living there. Magellan was so impressed by the sight that he called the islands Tierra Del Fuego, which means 'The Land of Fire'. It is not a very good name, because it is cold there.

Salt deposits in the Dead Sea

Map showing the location of Tierra del Fuego

Which great rock constantly changes colour?

One of the most impressive sights in Australia is Ayers Rock. It is a huge rock 348 metres high and 6 kilometres long. The rock stands like a mountain above the surrounding plain, and appears to change colour throughout the day. Its sandstone rock reflects the sunlight so that it looks gold, orange or red depending on the time of day.

Where is the Atlantic Ocean north of the Pacific Ocean?

The Atlantic Ocean is generally east of the Pacific Ocean. However the Panama Canal, which connects the two oceans, runs almost north-south, the Atlantic Ocean being at the northern end of the canal and the Pacific Ocean at the southern end.

The Panama Canal joins the Pacific and Atlantic Oceans.

Ayers Rock

Where does a river flow backwards over a waterfall?

This extraordinary sight can be seen in eastern Canada on the St John River. Just before the river enters the Bay of Fundy, it flows through a gorge and over a waterfall. The Bay of Fundy has the highest tide in the world and at high tide, water flows back *up* the river. The level rises above the waterfall, and the water flows back over it until the high tide passes. Because the flow reverses in this way, the falls are known as the Reversing Falls of St John.

Where are the antipodes?

The antipodes are two places on the Earth's surface that are directly opposite each other. If you could tunnel straight down through the centre of the Earth, you would come out at the antipodes. New Zealand is approximately at the antipodes to Britain, for example.

Where is the world's smallest country?

The world's smallest country is inside Rome, the capital city of Italy. It is the Vatican City, and it is governed by the Roman Catholic Church as an independent country. It is 0.44 square kilometres in area, and has a population of a thousand people. The whole country could be squeezed into a corner of any large city park.

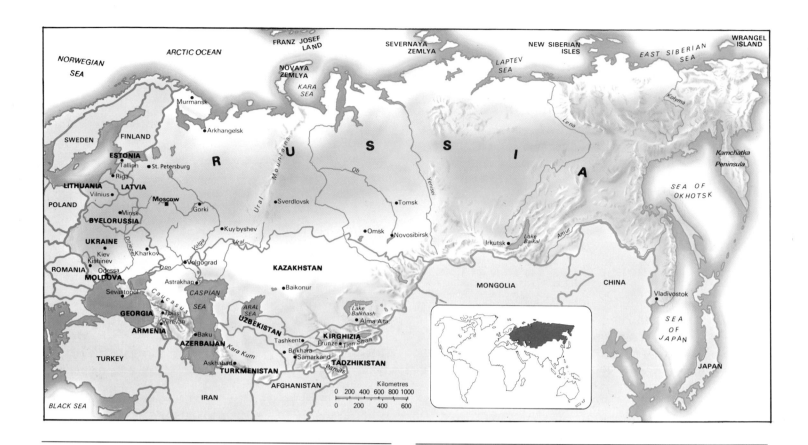

Which is the world's largest country?

The largest country in the world is Russia. It covers 17,075,000 square kilometres, nearly twice the size of the United States of America. The population is 148 million people.

Where is Sri Lanka?

Sri Lanka used to be called Ceylon. It is a large island off the south-east coast of India. Its capital is Colombo.

What is Dogger Bank?

Dogger Bank is a huge sandbank off the north-east coast of England in the North Sea. It is famous as a fishing ground.

What are the Roaring Forties?

This is the name given to the ocean region south of latitude 40°S where strong north-west to west winds blow constantly.

Where is 'The Land of the Midnight Sun'?

'The Land of the Midnight Sun' gets its name because, during the summer, the sun does not set for at least one day and there is no night. (During the winter, the opposite is true and the Sun does not rise, so there is no day). This happens in two places – the Arctic and the Antarctic. The midnight sun can be seen in the lands north of the Arctic Circle and south of the Antarctic Circle – the northern parts of Alaska, Canada, Greenland, Scandinavia and Russia, and Antarctica.

Where is the Black Forest?

The Black Forest is a thickly wooded mountainous region in West Germany separated from Switzerland by the River Rhine.

What is the Giant's Causeway?

This odd rock formation is in Northern Ireland. It consists of several thousand six-sided columns of rocks of varying height and has the appearance of giant steps.

What is Old Faithful?

Old Faithful is the name of a famous geyser in Yellowstone National Park in the United States. It gets its unusual name because it spouts regularly every hour, and has done so ever since it was discovered in 1870.

Where is Atlantis?

Atlantis is the name of an island on which there was supposed to have been a great civilization. According to legend, the island was in the Atlantic Ocean and it sank beneath the sea long ago. It is likely that this story is partly true, though Atlantis has nothing to do with the Atlantic Ocean. In the Aegean Sea in Greece, a volcanic island exploded in about 1645 BC. The centre of the island, which is now called Santorini or Thera, sank into the sea. Recently the remains of a rich civilization that was destroyed in the explosion have been found there. It is probable that such a catastrophic event would have been remembered in some way, and it could have given rise to the legend of Atlantis.

Old Faithful

Giant's Causeway, County Antrim, Northern Ireland

ANIMALS

What is the difference between an animal and a plant?

The main difference is that an animal can move and a plant stays in the same place all the time. Another difference is that animals eat other animals or plants for food, but most plants make their own food.

What is a family of animals?

When animal experts talk about a family of animals, they do not only mean parents and young. Different animals that have similar bodies are said to be in the same family. Wild cats such as lions, tigers and leopards, and pet cats all belong to the cat family.

Are people animals?

People are like animals such as monkeys and apes. We have the same kinds of bodies as these animals. It is likely that we are descended from similar animals, so we are animals too. However, people can use their brains to think up ways of altering their surroundings to suit themselves – by making buildings, for example. This kind of intelligent behaviour makes people different from other animals.

What great discovery about animals did Charles Darwin make?

Charles Darwin sailed around the world in the 1830s. From his observations of animals in many different places, he showed that one kind of animal can gradually change over many generations. This is called evolution.

How many different kinds of animals are there?

Animals are said to belong to different species if they cannot breed together and produce young that are able to breed. This is why the animals stay different. The total number of animal species is more than a million. More than half of all the species are insects.

Leopard

Why are such different animals as whales, bats and kangaroos all called mammals?

Animal experts think of animals that are generally alike as being in the same class. Fishes make up a class. So do insects, and birds. Mammals are the class of animals in which the mother feeds her young on her own milk. Whales, bats and kangaroos all raise their young in this way. They are therefore all members of the class of mammals, even though they look so different.

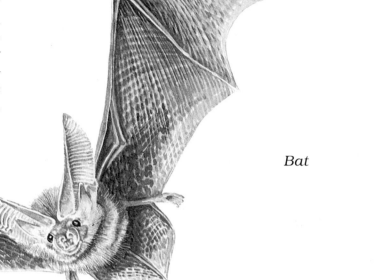

Bat

Kangaroo and joey

What are marsupials?

A marsupial is a special kind of mammal. Most mammals are born fully formed. Baby marsupials are born very tiny, and spend their early life inside a special pouch on their mother's body. Kangaroos and wallabies are marsupials.

What are monotremes?

Monotremes are mammals born from eggs like birds, but they are raised on milk like other mammals. The duck-billed platypus is a monotreme.

How many kinds of birds are there?

The total number of species of birds is about 8600.

What are feathers made of?

The feathers of a bird are made of the same thing as your nails and hair. This is a substance called keratin. A bird's beak is made of keratin too. The feathers and beak grow like our hair and nails. However, a bird does not have to cut its feathers and beak. Old feathers drop out, and the beak wears away as it grows so that it stays the same size.

Is a sea anemone a flower?

No, it is an animal that lives on the seabed and has spreading tentacles that look like flowers. The tentacles trap tiny animals or food particles to eat.

Which animal is most dangerous to people?

The most dangerous animals of all are the tiny arrow poison frogs of South America. The skin of one of these frogs contains the most powerful poison known. There is enough in each frog to kill hundreds of people. They are called arrow poison frogs because the Indians used the frogs to make poison-tipped arrows.

Arrow poison frog

Camel

Are any animals able to live without water?

Several animals manage to live in deserts, where there is no water to drink. We would quickly die of thirst, but small desert animals such as jerboas and kangaroo rats need much less water to live. They get all they need from the plants or animal food that they eat. They do not need to drink at all. Camels are able to cross desert areas because they can live without drinking for a long time. But they do need water, and drink a lot when they find it.

What is fur made of?

Fur is a thick covering of hair that covers many mammals. Usually the hair is fairly short. Air trapped inside the fur helps to keep the animals warm.

Why should people avoid a skunk?

Skunks are furry black animals with white stripes. They live in North America. If a skunk is frightened it defends itself by spraying its enemy with an evil-smelling fluid. The smell is terrible and it can last for days.

Which animal moves by changing shape?

Amoebas are tiny animals that look like blobs of jelly. They are so small that they can only be seen with a microscope. Amoebas live in water and in animals. They have no limbs, but are able to move by changing shape. The amoeba bulges out in one direction, forming a finger-shaped extension of its body. Then the rest of the body flows into the extension, moving slightly as it does so.

What is ivory?

Ivory is a hard creamy-white material that comes from the horns, teeth and tusks of animals. The best ivory comes from elephant tusks.

Why do some animals have no eyes?

Most animals need eyes to find food and avoid being caught. But animals like sponges and sea anemones take food that comes to them in the water. They are not pleasant to eat and have few enemies, so they do not need eyes. Many animals that live underground, especially cave animals, do not have eyes and are blind. There is no light where they live and eyes would be of no use to them.

Elephants

Why are some animals luminous?

Many animals that live in the dark can use their eyes. They may live in the dark depths of the sea, or prefer to be active at night. Some of them are luminous. They glow with light produced by chemicals in their bodies. Many deep-sea fish are luminous, and so are glow-worms and fireflies. The light may be a signal to their own kind, so that groups can keep together and the animals can find one another to breed.

Why does an elephant have such big ears?

Elephants have very large ears to help them keep cool! It is hot where they live, and the elephants fan out their ears to lose heat from their bodies.

Why do camels have humps?

Camels have one or two humps on their backs, and they act as stores of energy. The humps are made of fat, and the fat will provide the camel with energy if food is short.

Why do zebras and tigers have stripes?

Zebras and tigers are among the most distinctive animals in a zoo. Their stripes make them stand out. However, where they live, their stripes help to conceal them from their enemies – and their victims. Zebras live on grasslands and in mountains in Africa, and tigers in forests in Asia. Their stripes help them to merge with their surroundings and remain unseen.

Peacock butterfly

Emperor moth

Why do most insects have eyes with thousands of lenses?

Our eyes each have one lens to enable us to see. It is the clear section in the middle of the eye. Under a microscope, you can see that an insect's eye is usually made up of thousands of tiny lenses. It must see thousands of images of a scene instead of one as we do. However, this kind of vision easily shows up movement. It enables the insect to react fast and quickly seize its prey or escape danger. This is why it is difficult to hit a flying insect.

Why do some butterflies and moths have eyes on their wings?

Some butterflies and moths have large round spots on their wings that look like eyes. These can help the butterfly or moth to avoid being eaten. When a bird or other animal tries to attack the insect, it opens its wings as it flies off. This reveals the 'eyes', confusing the insect's enemy by making it think it has attacked something much bigger that has eyes. The enemy hesitates, and the insect escapes.

Zebras

How many legs do centipedes and millipedes have?

Centipedes and millipedes are long insect-like animals with many short legs under their bodies. They are not insects, but are related to them. Centipede means 'hundred feet' and millipede 'thousand feet'. In fact, centipedes have up to about 350 legs, and millipedes up to about twice as many.

Why does the peacock spread its tail?

The peacock is one of the most marvellous sights of the bird world. It raises the long feathers above its tail to make a huge fan of glossy blue-green plumes dotted with large eye-spots. The peacock is a male Indian peafowl. The peacock raises the fan to impress the peahen, and to encourage her to breed with him.

Peacock and peahen

What colour is a chameleon?

A chameleon can be almost any colour. This lizard changes colour to match the colour of its surroundings.

Why are some insects brightly coloured?

Many insects are decorated with bright colours, like the yellow and black stripes of wasps and bees. Also, many of these gaudy insects are poisonous or have stings. The colours are a warning to birds and other animals that they should be left alone.

Biggest, Fastest, Tallest, Smallest

Swift

How swift is the fastest animal?

The fastest animals are swift in more ways than one. They are the birds called swifts. The spine-tailed swift, which lives in Asia, can fly through the air at a speed of more than 160 kilometres an hour. It could keep up with an express train travelling at top speed.

Which is the biggest animal in the world?

The biggest animal that has ever lived is the blue whale. It may grow to more than 30 metres in length, and weighs about 160 tonnes when fully grown. Blue whales have been hunted by whalers and are now rare.

Which is the tallest animal?

The tallest animal in the world is the giraffe. A giraffe may look down from a height of as much as 6 metres – as high as a two-storey house.

How small is the smallest animal?

The smallest animals are protozoans, so tiny that they can only be seen with a powerful microscope. Some protozoans are so small that 5000 of them would measure only one centimetre.

Cheetah

Which animal can run faster than any other?

The champion athlete of the world's land animals is the cheetah. This wild cat can sprint at a speed of up to 100 kilometres an hour over a short distance. It reaches such speeds when chasing antelopes over the African grasslands.

How long can animals live?

Few animals live longer than human beings, but one animal outstrips our lifespan by far. This is the giant tortoise. It is possible that giant tortoises can live for as long as 200 years.

Which is the slowest mammal in the world?

The slowest mammal in the world is the three-toed sloth which moves at the rate of 100 metres an hour.

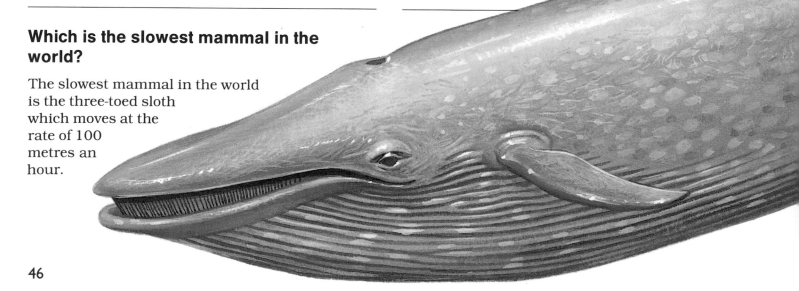

How small is the smallest bird?

The smallest bird is so tiny that it weighs only as much as a lump of sugar. It is a tiny hummingbird called a bee hummingbird, because its body is about the same size as a bee. Even with its long beak and tail, it measures only 6 centimetres long. The bee hummingbird lives in Cuba.

How far do birds migrate?

The world's greatest traveller is the Arctic tern, which migrates between the Arctic and the Antarctic and back every year! Each journey may be as much as 19,000 kilometres long.

How high can birds fly?

People climbing Mount Everest have seen birds at a height of 8000 metres. Birds have also been seen from aircraft flying this high.

Ostrich

Can the world's largest bird fly?

The world's largest bird is much too big to fly. It is the ostrich, which lives on the grasslands of Africa. It may stand more than $2\frac{1}{2}$ metres high, and weigh 150 kilograms or more.

Blue whale

How long is the longest snake?

The longest snake is the reticulated python or regal python, which lives in South-East Asia. It may grow to a length of 10 metres. It is not poisonous, but hugs its victims to death. The python coils its long body around its prey to stop it breathing.

Which bird has the longest wings?

The wandering albatross has the longest wingspan of any bird. Its wings may measure more than $3\frac{1}{2}$ metres across.

Which animal has the longest nose?

The longest nose of any animal measures about 2 metres long – as big as a very tall person. It belongs, of course, to the elephant. The elephant has more uses for its nose or trunk than breathing and smelling. It can suck up water in the trunk and give itself a shower, use it to carry food to its mouth, and grip its enemies in a fight.

How Animals Live

Gorillas

Are gorillas savage animals?

Gorillas certainly look savage. They stand as high as an adult person, and weigh about twice as much. To threaten, the gorilla beats its chest with its long powerful arms. This looks frightening, but gorillas are really very peaceful. They live only on plants, and do not fight each other.

How long can a whale stay under water?

Whales are mammals, like ourselves, and breathe air. They hold their breath under water, and come to the surface to gulp fresh air into their lungs. Sperm whales make deep dives to capture sharks and giant squids for food. They can stay down for at least an hour, and possibly for as long as two hours.

Why do birds sing?

Birds normally sing for two good reasons – to appeal to other birds or to threaten them. It is usually the male bird that sings. He sings to call a female bird to become his mate and have young together. However, the song is also a warning to other male birds to stay away.

Are any animals able to talk?

Parrots and mynah birds can talk to us. But these birds do not understand what they are saying. They merely copy what we teach them. However, scientists have taught a sign language to chimpanzees. They believe that the chimpanzees understand how to use the language, and can 'talk' with us in signs.

How does a flying squirrel fly without wings?

In the forests of Asia, northern Europe and North America, there are squirrels that can fly through the air. They usually fly only at night, and swoop from tree to tree in search of food. As they launch themselves into the air, the squirrels spread out a web of furry skin between the front legs and back legs. The web is like a parachute, and enables the squirrels to glide through the air.

Hummingbird

Why do many animals sleep through winter?

You do not see many animals during the winter because they have hidden away somewhere and are asleep. This winter sleep is called hibernation. Frogs, toads, lizards, snakes, bats, mice, hedgehogs, squirrels, insects such as butterflies and even bears may all hibernate. They do so because food is so hard to find in winter that they would starve. In their deep sleep, they need very little food to stay alive. They can eat enough before hibernation to keep alive during the winter.

A brown bear in hibernation

Which birds can fly backwards?

Tiny hummingbirds can hover in the air in front of a flower to suck out the nectar. To leave, the bird simply flies backwards. No other bird can do this.

Can any birds use tools?

A few birds use objects to help them rather as we use simple tools. The woodpecker finch of the Galapagos Islands takes a cactus spine in its beak, and uses it to get insects out of holes. The song thrush breaks open snail shells by hitting them against a rock.

How can bats fly through the dark?

Bats sleep during the day and emerge at night to find fruit or catch insects to eat. They can find their way in total darkness. Instead of using their eyes, they use their ears. The bats make high squeaking noises as they fly through the dark. These sounds bounce off any obstacles or food ahead of them, and the bats hear the echoes of the squeaks. From the echoes, they can tell exactly where they are flying – even though it is completely dark!

Anaconda

How are some birds able to dive and swim under water?

Penguins are the birds that are most at home under water. They cannot fly and use their wings like flippers to swim, while steering with their feet.

Emperor penguin and chick

How do snakes move?

A snake has no legs, but it can move quickly. It crawls over the ground in several ways. The snake usually bends its body into curves. It pushes against the ground on the outsides of the curves and moves itself forward. It may also move by bending its body into loops and then straightening itself.

Do fishes breathe under water?

Yes. All animals, whether they live in water or in air, need oxygen to live. Oxygen is one of the gases in the air, and we take oxygen into our lungs every time we breathe in. There it goes into our blood to keep us alive. Fishes breathe oxygen too. The oxygen is dissolved in the water. As a fish sucks water into its gills, the oxygen goes from the water into the fish's blood.

Kiwi

Do flightless birds have wings?

Although they cannot fly, flightless birds do have wings and some make use of their wings. However, the kiwi's wings are only 5 centimetres long, and are completely hidden beneath its feathers so that it does not appear to have any wings. Penguins, on the other hand, have prominent wings that they use as flippers to swim.

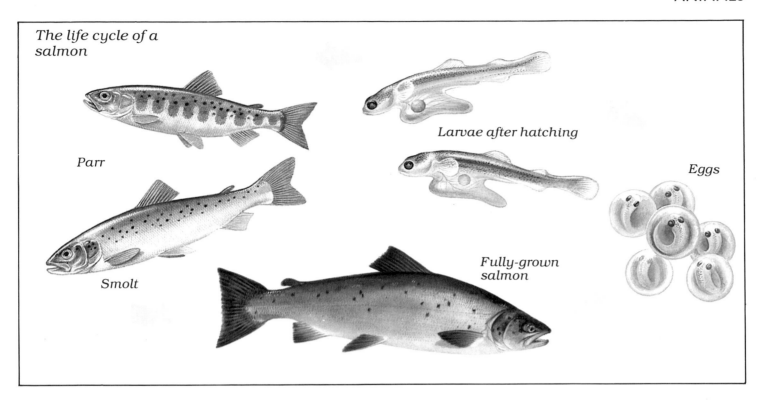

The life cycle of a salmon

Parr

Smolt

Larvae after hatching

Eggs

Fully-grown salmon

How does a salmon return to its birthplace?

Salmon are born in pools, streams or in the rushing waters of a river. When they grow up, which may take several years, they swim downstream to the sea. They live in the sea for a year or more, feeding and growing, and then swim back to where they were born and have young. The salmon may swim 1600 kilometres out to sea, yet it can still find its birthplace. The salmon often has a difficult journey home. It has to swim against fast currents and it will even jump over waterfalls to get there. The fish probably uses the Sun to guide itself through the sea to the right river mouth. Then it probably sniffs its way back home, using its sense of smell to lead it back up-river until it reaches its birthplace. At the end of the journey the salmon is thin, pale and very tired.

How do some fishes make electricity?

About 250 kinds of fishes can produce electric shocks. They do this to find their way in muddy water, and also to kill their prey. The most powerful electric fishes can produce shocks of several hundred volts – enough to stun a person. They have special muscles that work like batteries.

How does a flying fish fly?

A flying fish takes to the air to avoid being caught by a bigger fish or to avoid a boat. It swims along the surface, beating its tail to get up speed, and then spreads its fins like wings and soars into the air at about 60 kilometres an hour. It glides over the waves, using its tail to propel itself back into the air if necessary.

Flying fish

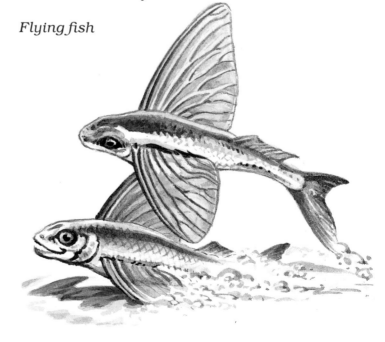

Water spiders

Which spider lives under water?

Spiders breathe air, and yet one spider spends its life under water. It does this by swimming down, and weaving a little chamber of silk among some water plants. Then it carries down bubbles of air to fill the chamber. There the water spider lives, lying in wait. When a water insect or some other small creature comes near, the spider dashes out to catch it and bring it back to the chamber to eat.

How far away can one moth smell another?

At breeding time, the female moth produces a scent to attract the male. The male moth can detect this scent as far as 11 kilometres away.

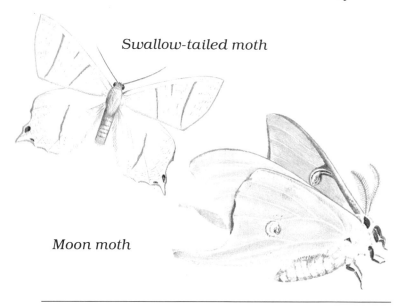

Swallow-tailed moth

Moon moth

Where do bees go in the winter?

Honeybees spend the winter in their hive, living on the honey made from nectar collected during the summer. Bumblebees are different. The whole colony dies as winter comes, except for the queen bee. She hibernates through the winter and founds a new colony the following spring.

How do honeybees tell each other where to find food?

Honeybees can tell each other where to find nectar, the food they take from flowers. A bee that discovers some nectar flies back to the hive, and then does a little dance before the other bees. The dance is like a figure eight. The direction of the figure tells the other bees where the nectar is in relation to the Sun. Also, the faster the bee dances, the nearer the nectar is to the hive.

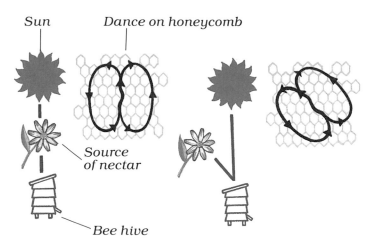

Sun *Dance on honeycomb*

Source of nectar

Bee hive

Honeybees

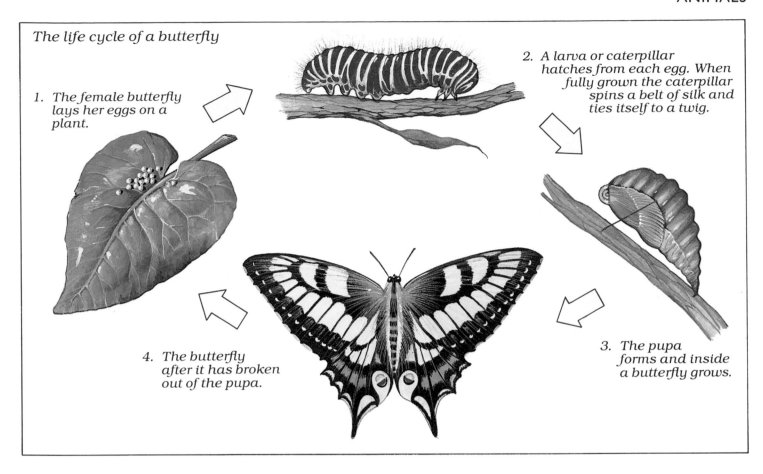

The life cycle of a butterfly

1. The female butterfly lays her eggs on a plant.

2. A larva or caterpillar hatches from each egg. When fully grown the caterpillar spins a belt of silk and ties itself to a twig.

3. The pupa forms and inside a butterfly grows.

4. The butterfly after it has broken out of the pupa.

How does a caterpillar turn into a butterfly?

A caterpillar is a young butterfly. The caterpillar hatches from an egg, and spends its life eating and growing until it is ready to change into its adult form, the butterfly. But first it grows a hard case around its body. In this form, it is called a pupa or chrysalis. Inside, the caterpillar's body breaks down and the butterfly grows. This change is caused by substances called hormones in the body. After a few days or weeks, the case splits open and the butterfly emerges. At first the butterfly's wings are only little pads, but then they flatten and expand. After a short time the butterfly can fly away.

How do insects breathe?

Most insects breathe air, but they do not have nostrils in their heads as we do to breathe through. Instead, they have holes along the sides of their bodies. From the holes, little tubes extend through the insect's body to carry the air to all parts of it.

Where does a dragonfly spend most of its life?

Although you see dragonflies flying through the air, they spend most of their lives under water. The dragonflies are in the adult stage of their lives, which lasts only a few weeks. Before becoming adults, they may spend several years living under water as nymphs. The nymphs are like the adult insects but have no wings.

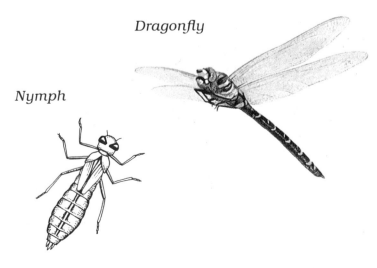

Dragonfly

Nymph

Where Animals Live

What kinds of animals live at the bottom of the ocean?

Some very unusual fishes live in the ocean depths. It is so deep that it is totally dark, and many of the fishes are luminous. This helps them to find each other to breed. Hunting for food is difficult in the blackness, and many fishes have long needle-sharp teeth to help them make a catch.

Where do sponges come from?

Sponges are animals that live at the bottom of the sea and lakes. They are fixed to rocks.

Why are the animals in Australia and New Zealand different from animals elsewhere?

Australia is the main home of marsupials such as kangaroos and wallabies. New Zealand also has many strange and interesting animals, especially birds such as kiwis and flesh-eating and flightless parrots. Animals are generally different there because these places are separated from the large continents by the ocean. Different animals evolved there and could not spread elsewhere.

How do moles live underground?

Moles tunnel under the ground, hunting creatures such as worms and grubs. Their homes are in burrows underground. In fields, you can often see molehills, which are little mounds of earth left where moles have burrowed through the ground. They can tunnel easily. They have narrow heads and strong front claws to thrust their way through the soil.

Where did the dodo live?

The dodo lived on the island of Mauritius in the Indian Ocean. It was a big fat bird with a large hooked beak, tiny wings and a little curly tail. The dodo could not fly, and it was hunted by the sailors that landed on Mauritius. It soon died out and, as no dodos lived elsewhere, it became extinct. When we talk about something being extinct, we often say that it is 'as dead as a dodo'.

Which animal builds a dam?

The beaver is a remarkable animal which is found in North America and part of Europe and Asia. It is a rodent like a rat, but much bigger. Beavers live by rivers, and some make their home in a hole in the bank. The hole has an underwater entrance, and the beavers can swim in and out. Other beavers build their own homes, which are called lodges. They cut down trees by chewing them, and make a dam across the river with the logs. They then build a lodge by felling more trees, and piling them up in the middle of the pond formed by the dam. The lodge is packed with mud and has an underwater entrance.

Beavers building a lodge

Where do birds of paradise live?

Birds of paradise live in the forests of New Guinea and northern Australia. They have marvellous plumage of brilliant colours. The birds of paradise got their strange name because they are so beautiful.

Where does coral grow?

Coral reefs and pieces of coral are formed by tiny animals like sea anemones. The coral animals have stony or horny skeletons. Many live in colonies, and the skeletons grow together in unusual shapes. Some look like plants or flowers. Corals live in all oceans, but in warm tropical waters they can form huge colonies called coral reefs. These reefs lie offshore just below the water at the coast and around islands. The Great Barrier Reef in Australia is over 2000 kilometres long.

Why do barnacles and limpets stick themselves to rocks?

Animals that live on rocky seashores have to spend their lives in and out of water as the tide rises and falls. Limpets and barnacles are suited to this life. When the tide is low and they are in the air, they close their shells tightly around their bodies. This stops the moist bodies from drying up. They open up and feed when the water covers them. Limpets crawl over rocks, grazing on the tiny plants that live there. Barnacles wave tentacles in the water to capture food.

Birds of paradise

Polar bear

Do lions and tigers live in the same countries?

Tigers live only in Asia. Lions live mainly in Africa. There are also a few lions in north-west India. So India is the only country which has both lions and tigers.

Where do polar bears live?

Polar bears live only in the Arctic, around the North Pole.

Animal Homes

Which bird sews its nest together?

Several birds of southern Asia and Australia are so good at sewing that they are called tailor birds. They make their nests by stitching leaves together to make a cup, which they then line with soft cotton or grass. The tailor bird punches holes along the edges of the leaves with its beak. Then it takes a plant fibre or piece of spider's web and threads it through the holes. Finally, it pulls the leaves together and knots the thread.

Why does the hermit crab have to change its home?

Hermit crabs do not have hard shells like ordinary crabs. To protect themselves, they squeeze their bodies into empty seashells. However, the crabs grow. They soon find their homes too small, and have to seek a bigger shell.

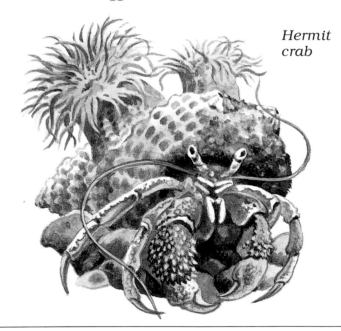

Hermit crab

Which animal carries its home around?

The snail carries its home on its back in the form of a shell. If danger threatens, the snail can pull its soft body right into the shell. Seashells like whelks live in the same way.

Tailor birds

Which animal hides under a trapdoor?

Trapdoor spiders burrow into the ground, lining the hole with silk and making a hinged lid of silk and soil to close it. Over the lid, the spider places mosses or other plants so that it cannot be seen. Beneath the trapdoor, the spider lies in wait. As soon as an insect comes near, the spider rushes from its hideaway and seizes its victim.

Which bird paints its home?

To attract a female bird, the male bower bird makes a construction of twigs called a bower. To make the bower attractive, the bird may decorate it with flowers and other colourful objects. Some bower birds go even further, and daub a kind of paint on their bowers. They may make the paint from the coloured juices of berries, or by mixing charcoal from burnt bushes with their saliva. As a brush, the bird holds a piece of bark in its beak. Bower birds live in the tropical forests of New Guinea and Australia.

Animals and their Young

Mouthbrooder

Which animal lays the most eggs?

Wild birds such as tits and pheasants can lay up to about 15 eggs in a nest, and chickens can lay hundreds in a year. But this is nothing compared to fishes, which may lay thousands or even millions of eggs.

Which animal carries its eggs on its back?

Most frogs lay their eggs in water. The eggs hatch into tadpoles, which change into frogs. Some frogs can breed without water. The eggs are placed in pouches on the frog's back, and hatch there. The tadpoles may then be placed in water, or they may stay on their parent's back until they become frogs.

Which bird holds its egg on its feet?

It is so cold in Antarctica that penguins dare not place their single eggs on the ground. To stop its egg freezing, the penguin carries it on its feet and lowers a fold of warm fur over it.

How big is a baby whale?

Blue whales are the largest animals that have ever lived, and they have the biggest babies. A baby blue whale is $7\frac{1}{2}$ metres long when it is born – as big as a house.

Which fish shelters its young in its mouth?

Most fishes lay eggs. Many lay huge numbers of eggs and abandon them in the water, expecting a few to hatch. Others lay few eggs, but take care of them. These include fishes known as mouthbrooders, which keep their eggs and young fishes in their mouths for safety. Somehow they manage to eat without swallowing their eggs or young.

Which animal makes a nest of bubbles?

Several frogs and fishes make nests of bubbles or foam for their eggs. The Siamese fighting fish, which lives in rivers and lakes in South-East Asia, is a good example. At breeding time, the male blows bubbles from its mouth to form a floating raft of bubbles. The female fighting fish then lays the eggs, and the male places them among the bubbles. The bubbles shelter the eggs, but the male guards them as well until they hatch.

Siamese fighting fish

Weapons and Defences

Armadillo

Which animal is covered in armour?

Many animals have hard coverings on their bodies, but one particular animal looks as if it is covered in armour. This is the armadillo. It lives in Central and South America. The armadillo has hard plates of bone over its body. If it is attacked, it rolls itself into a ball. It is completely protected, like a knight in armour.

Which animal vanishes in a smoke screen?

Octopuses, squid and cuttlefishes can all escape danger by disappearing in a kind of smoke screen. If they are attacked, they squirt some dark ink into the water. The ink spreads out in a cloud like a smoke screen, and the octopus, squid or cuttlefish can escape unharmed.

Are all snakes poisonous?

There are about 3000 kinds of snakes, but only about 300 of them are harmful to people. Of these snakes, very few have poison strong enough to kill.

Which animal comes to pieces?

Some lizards can escape their enemies by coming to pieces when they are captured. If they are grabbed by their tails, the tail comes off and the lizard scuttles away to safety. A new tail soon grows to replace the old one.

Which birds play tricks on their enemies?

Several birds known as waders may defend their young by playing tricks on their enemies. They include curlews and plovers. If a dangerous animal such as a fox approaches the nest, which is on the ground, the parent bird leaves the nest and its young. It drags one wing as if it is broken. The enemy turns away and begins to follow the parent bird, thinking it has an easy victim. The parent bird leads the hunter a safe distance from the nest, and then gives up its pretence and flies away.

Killdeer nest

Fox

Killdeer

Which animals look exactly like bark, twigs and leaves?

Some insects that live in bushes and trees copy their surroundings so exactly that they do not look like insects at all. Leaf insects have green bodies shaped like leaves, some caterpillars have bodies that are exactly the shape and colour of twigs, and some moths have wings with patterns that look just like bark. If danger threatens, these insects keep very still and avoid detection.

Getting Food

Which insects are farmers?

Leafcutter ants, which live in America, cut up leaves and carry the pieces into their underground homes. There they chew up the leaves to make a compost on which the ants grow a particular kind of fungus. The ants harvest the fungus from their gardens and eat it. Pastoral ants are like dairy farmers. They look after 'herds' of greenfly and blackfly in order to gather the sweet honeydew that these insects produce.

Which animal uses a fishing rod?

Several fishes catch other fishes by fishing for them! Among them is the anglerfish. It has a pole-like spike sticking out of its head with a flap on the end. The fish lies on the bottom of the ocean, and waves the flap to and fro. This lure attracts other fishes which are then seized by the angler.

Why do some birds ride on animals?

In Africa, oxpeckers ride on the backs of cattle and of large wild animals like the rhinoceros. The giant cowbird rides on cattle in Central and South America. These birds eat pests that live in the animals' skins. This helps to clean the animals as well as feed the birds.

Oxpeckers on a rhinoceros

Barn owl

How can owls hunt at night?

Most owls sleep during the day and hunt for mice and other small woodland creatures at night. They swoop through the trees in what would seem to be complete darkness to us. However, the owl's big eyes are much more sensitive to light than ours. They can still see. Also, owls have very sharp hearing and can locate their prey by the rustling noises it makes. Owls are able to fly silently and surprise their victims.

What do seashells eat?

Seashells close up tight when they are out of the water. But when the tide comes in and covers them, the shells open and they can feed. Some seashell animals put out rough tongues with which they scrape at plants like seaweeds. Others extend tubes that suck in sea water, and the animals eat particles of food floating in the water.

How do bees make honey?

Bees collect a liquid called nectar from flowers. Nectar contains sugars, like the sugar we use in food. The bee takes the nectar back to its hive, where it is placed in a honeycomb. The bees fan the honeycomb with their wings to make water evaporate and turn the nectar into honey. The honeycomb is the bee's food store, but we take it to get honey.

Animal Differences

Dolphin

Porpoise

What is the difference between a dolphin and a porpoise?

Dolphins and porpoises are large animals that live in the sea and also in rivers. They are in fact small whales, and they have to come to the surface to breathe as whales do. Dolphins have a snout or beak containing as many as 200 teeth, but porpoises have blunt heads without a snout or beak.

How can you tell a seal from a sea-lion?

There are two main differences between a seal and a sea-lion. A sea-lion has ears, and a seal has no ears. In addition, a sea-lion can move on land by using all of its four flippers, but a seal can only drag itself forward with its two front flippers.

What is the difference between an insect and a spider?

The main difference is that insects have six legs and spiders have eight legs. There are other differences too. Many insects have wings, unlike spiders, and many spiders weave webs, unlike insects.

What is the difference between an alligator and a crocodile?

You can tell an alligator from a crocodile by looking at its head. An alligator has a broad, rounded snout whereas the snout of a crocodile is thinner and more pointed. Also, the teeth are slightly different. The large fourth tooth on each side of the lower jaw can be seen outside the jaw when a crocodile closes its mouth. When an alligator closes its mouth, the tooth is hidden inside the jaw. Wild alligators live only in small areas of the United States and China. Crocodiles are much more common.

What is the difference between a tortoise and a turtle?

Usually, a tortoise lives on land and a turtle lives in water. However, in America, most of these animals are called turtles.

What is the difference between a frog and a toad?

You can tell a frog from a toad by its skin. In general, a frog has a moist, smooth and shiny skin, whereas the skin of a toad is dry, dull and rough or covered with warts. Also, frogs are usually good at jumping and toads are not.

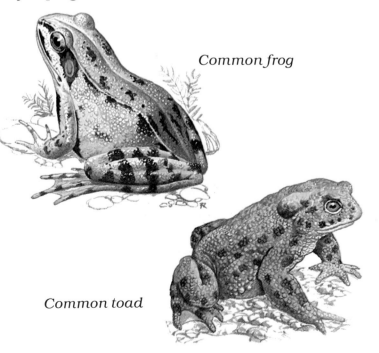

Common frog

Common toad

Animal Names

Seahorse

What is a pride of lions?

A pride is a group of lions that live together. It is not always a family of two parents and their young. There may be several adult lions and lionesses with all their cubs. Each pride has its own piece of land or territory.

What is a bush baby?

Bush babies are graceful little furry animals with huge eyes and hands and feet that both look like human hands. They live in forests in Africa. During the day, bush babies hide away and huddle together to sleep. They come out at night, leaping through the trees to find insects to eat. The largest bush baby is no bigger than a squirrel.

What kind of animal is a giant panda?

The giant panda is a rare and unusual animal. It lives in remote parts of China, and feeds mainly on bamboo shoots. It looks like a medium-sized black-and-white bear. In fact, it is not a bear at all, but is related to the raccoon.

Panda

What kind of animal is a seahorse?

A seahorse is a very strange animal. It lives in the sea, and its head looks like a horse's head. But it is much smaller than a horse, being no more than 15 centimetres long. It has a curly tail, no legs and swims in an upright position, using a fin on its back. The fin gives it away, for the seahorse is in fact a very unusual kind of fish.

How did woodpeckers get their name?

Woodpeckers deserve their name. They work at wood just as a carpenter does. You can hear their *rat-a-tat-tat* as they chisel away at a tree trunk, using their beaks to carve out holes in the wood. The woodpeckers make their nests in the holes. They also peck more lightly to pull insects out of the bark.

Prehistoric Animals

When did the first animals appear on Earth?

The first animals appeared about 2000 million years ago. They lived in the sea. They were protozoans, a name that comes from Greek words meaning 'first animals'. Protozoans are the simplest animals. They consist of a single, tiny living cell. Protozoans are now found in fresh water as well as the sea, and also in soil and in blood.

When was the Age of Dinosaurs?

Dinosaurs were reptiles, but very different from today's reptiles. Many were giant-sized, and armed with ferocious teeth and savage horns. Above them great pterosaurs swooped through the air on leathery wings. The dinosaurs and pterosaurs ruled the Earth from about 200 million years ago until they died out about 65 million years ago.

What did dinosaurs eat?

Many dinosaurs, including the biggest of all, *Diplodocus*, lived only on plants. Others were flesh-eaters, and hunted the plant-eating dinosaurs. Such huge creatures as *Diplodocus* were probably safe, even from monsters like *Tyrannosaurus*, which stood 6 metres high and had vast crocodile-like jaws. Many plant-eating dinosaurs protected themselves with armour. *Stegosaurus* had sharp plates along its back and a spiked tail to fend off flesh-eaters.

Diplodocus

How big was the largest dinosaur?

The biggest dinosaurs were the biggest land animals of all time. They included *Brachiosaurus* and *Diplodocus*, about 25 metres long. Even bigger was *Supersaurus*, which may have been 42 metres long and weighed 50 tonnes. These huge animals were plant-eaters and so not dangerous.

When did sabre-toothed tigers roam the land?

One of the most feared enemies of prehistoric people was the sabre-toothed tiger. This wild cat first roamed the land about 40 million years ago. Its jaws were armed with two long curved teeth that make it look more savage than today's tigers.

How do we know about prehistoric animals?

We know that prehistoric animals once lived on Earth because of their fossils. Fossils are the remains of animals and plants that lived millions of years ago. After the animals and plants died, they were buried in mud, sand or other materials that later turned into stone. In many cases, the remains turned to stone as well.

Where were mammoths preserved whole?

Mammoths were elephant-like creatures with huge curved tusks. They lived thousands of years ago. Whole bodies of mammoths have been found in Siberia. It is so cold there that the animals were frozen as soon as they died. Their bodies have remained unchanged, stored in a natural deep-freeze ever since.

How big was the first horse?

The first prehistoric animal that was like a horse was a creature called *Eohippus*. It lived in forests about 50 million years ago. *Eohippus* looked like a horse, and today's horses are its descendants. But it was only about 28 centimetres high – the size of a small dog!

Which fish is a living fossil?

A fish known as the coelacanth is often called a living fossil. This is because it was thought to be a prehistoric fish that had died out about 60 million years ago. It was known only as a fossil. Then a coelacanth was discovered in the Indian Ocean off South Africa in 1938. The fish had not died out, but was still alive. Furthermore, it was just like its fossil ancestors. Several more of these living fossils have since been found.

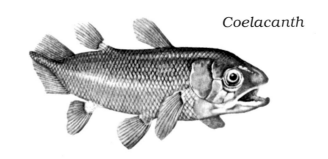

Coelacanth

Why are there no longer any dinosaurs or other prehistoric animals?

Almost all animals and plants gradually change as generations die and others are born. This is called evolution. Most prehistoric animals no longer exist because their descendants have changed into other kinds of animals. But some kinds died out and had no descendants. The great dinosaurs and pterosaurs died out about 65 million years ago, probably because it became too cold for them.

Eohippus

PLANTS

Do all plants have leaves?

Most, but not all, plants have leaves, though they do not always look like leaves. The blades of grass are leaves. Mushrooms and other fungi do not have leaves; nor do algae such as seaweeds, and lichens. Leaves help plants to breathe and to grow.

Does seaweed have roots?

Seaweed does not have roots. Seaweed is an alga and algae have neither flowers nor roots. Seaweed usually clings to stones, rocks, shells and break-waters with a holdfast which anchors it. Although the holdfast looks like roots, the seaweed does not feed through the holdfast as a plant feeds through its roots. Instead the seaweed takes food from the water in which it is growing.

Why does bladderwrack have bladders?

Bladderwrack is a very common brown seaweed. It grows on rocks which are usually covered by water when the tide comes in. It has flat stems with pairs of bladders which are filled with air. These bladders help the seaweed to float up from the rocks when they are covered by the sea. Other seaweeds have bladders to help them float and they will pop like small balloons if you squeeze them.

Do mosses have flowers?

No. Mosses have leaves and stems but no flowers. They sometimes look as if they are blooming, but the 'flower' is really a little capsule full of spores on the end of a stalk or leafy stem.

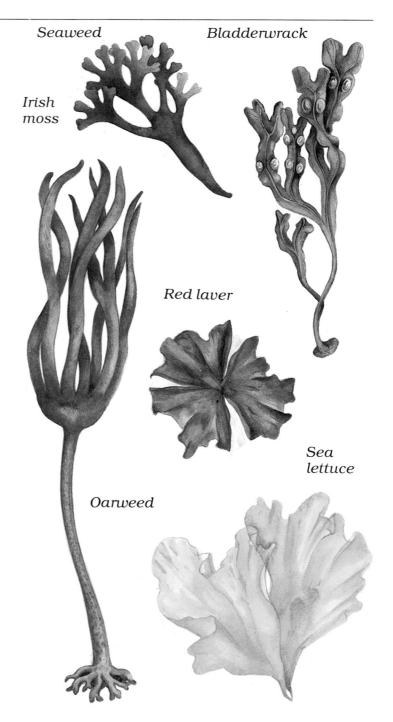

Seaweed

Bladderwrack

Irish moss

Red laver

Oarweed

Sea lettuce

White waterlily

How do the leaves of a waterlily float?

Waterlilies often have large leaves with many air spaces on the underside. The air trapped beneath the leaf makes it float on the water. Also, the leaves usually have strong stems which help them to keep upright. In this way, the waterlily exposes its leaves to the light it needs to stay alive.

Why do some plants trap insects?

Insect-eating plants often live in marshes and jungles where they cannot get all the food they need from the soil. They catch and eat small insects instead. Some insect-eating plants catch their prey with sticky leaves. Others, like the Venus flytrap of North Carolina and Florida in the United States, have hinged leaves which spring together when an insect lands on them.

Why do some plants have thorns?

Thorns, prickles and sharp spines help to protect a plant from hungry animals. They may also stop insects boring into the plant. Cows in a meadow will eat grass but not thistles, because they have too many spines. Sometimes seeds are prickly so that they will cling to an animal's fur and so get spread around.

Why does a stinkhorn stink?

A stinkhorn is a kind of fungus which stinks in order to attract flies. It may smell nasty to us, but flies like it. They feed on the slime which contains spores and then they carry the spores away on their legs. In this way stinkhorns can spread over a large area.

How do nettles sting?

Some kinds of nettles have sharp hairs on them that stick into you if you touch them. As they stick in, they inject a stinging liquid called formic acid. The nettle does this to try to stop animals eating it.

Pitcher plant

Venus flytrap

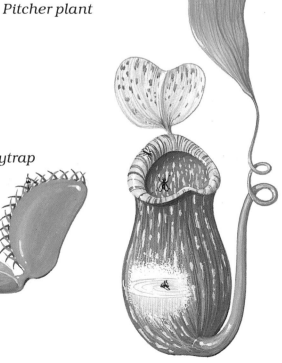

Hop

Male flowers

Fruit

Female flower

What are hops used for?

Hops are used for making beer. The flowers are like cones and are collected in the autumn when they are ripe. The scale-like petals are added to beer. They make it clear, help it to keep longer and give it a bitter flavour.

Are all plants in the nightshade family poisonous?

Deadly nightshade is famous because it is very poisonous. However, other plants of the night-shade family are not poisonous – in fact, we even eat some of them. The nightshades belong to a family of plants called Solanaceae. This family includes potatoes, tomatoes and tobacco.

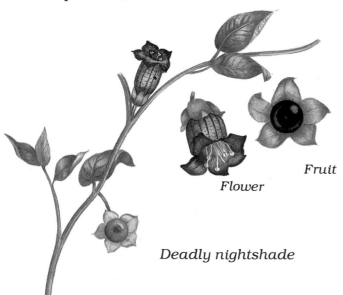

Fruit

Flower

Deadly nightshade

Why are many plants green?

Many plants are green because they contain a green pigment called chlorophyll. The chlorophyll enables a plant to make its own food. The green cells in a plant absorb energy from sunlight. This energy changes moisture from the soil and air, and carbon dioxide from the air, into foods such as sugar and starch which the plant needs for growth.

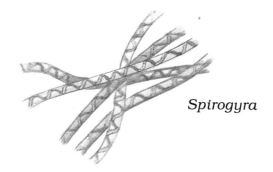

Spirogyra

What causes the green slime sometimes seen on ponds?

It is caused by huge numbers of very tiny plants called algae. Algae are the simplest kinds of plants, and they have no flowers and no roots. The most common alga on ponds is *Spirogyra*. If you examine a *Spirogyra* plant through a microscope, it looks like a spiral or spring. It produces vast numbers of spores that swim away from the parent plant and grow into new plants. In this way, a green slime of algae builds up on the pond.

What plant is used to make linen?

Linen is the oldest known textile and it is made from the stems of the flax plant which grows all over the world. Linen gets its name from the Latin name for flax, which is *linum*. It is made by soaking the flax stems until the soft part rots away. The hard fibres are then formed into yarn for weaving. The seeds of flax are used to make linseed oil.

Why is marram grass planted on sand dunes?

It is planted because it helps to stop the sand dunes blowing away. Marram grass has long rooting stems, which hold the sand together. Its leaves roll up in dry weather to keep in moisture, and open up in wet weather. When its roots have bound one layer of sand, the grass grows up through the next layer and grows another lot of roots.

Dog rose

Apple

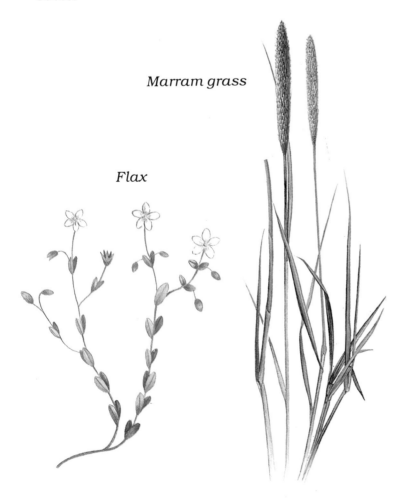

Marram grass

Flax

In what way are apples like roses?

Apples belong to a large family of plants that is called the Rosaceae after the roses. Plants in the same family have a certain feature that is alike in all of them. All the plants of the rose family have similar flowers, even though they may be very different in other ways. In fact, other fruits, such as strawberries, pears, plums and blackberries also belong to the rose family.

Can coconuts float?

Yes. The fruit of a coconut is covered with a thick, fibrous shell that floats. Coconut palms grow in warm regions, usually by the sea. A coconut will not start to grow unless it is soaked first. When they are ripe, the coconuts fall from the palm tree and drop or roll into the sea. They may float for several months before they drift ashore on a different coast and start to grow.

How Plants Grow

How do plants feed?

Plants have to feed themselves to stay alive, just as people and animals do. However, green plants are able to make their own food. They make sugars and starches by absorbing carbon dioxide through their leaves, and water from the soil and rain through their roots and leaves. They use energy from sunlight to change the gas and water into food, which they can store if necessary. This food-making process is called photosynthesis. The plants also take up minerals through their roots. Not all plants make their own food. They feed on other plants, or on the remains of plants. These plants are called parasite or saprophyte plants, and they include fungi such as mushrooms and toadstools.

How are insects useful to plants?

Insects are useful to plants because they carry pollen from one flower to another. A plant must be pollinated before it can form seeds. Insects are attracted to flowers by their bright colours, or by their smell, and by the sweet nectar many flowers produce. Some flowers even look like the insects they want to attract to them. As the insects reach for the nectar, they brush against the flower's stamens and stigmas and the pollen falls on to them. When they go to another flower, the pollen is brushed on to its stigmas.

Do cacti only grow in dry places?

Most cacti grow in dry places, but not all do. Some grow in rain forests, like the Christmas cactus of South America.

Why do desert plants often have thick, fleshy leaves?

Plants that live in dry places need to hold water for a very long time. They may have thick fleshy leaves to help them to store water. These leaves often have a waterproof surface to stop the moisture getting out. Many cacti do not have real leaves at all. They have fleshy stems which store moisture, and their leaves have changed into prickles.

Desert plants

Yucca

Creosote bush

Prickly pear

Lithops

Stapelia

Barrel cactus

Mesembryanthemum

How do climbing plants climb?

Plants climb in different ways. Some, like clematis, are very weak and have twisting stems which climb up other stronger plants. As the stems touch the other plants they grow more quickly on one side and so curl around the other plant. Some plants, like ivy, grow small roots on their stems and these help them to grow up walls. Peas and marrows have special coiled tendrils which wind around a support. Virginia creeper has little pads like suckers which cling to a wall or other surface. Climbing roses and blackberries use their sharp spines to hold on to surfaces or other plants.

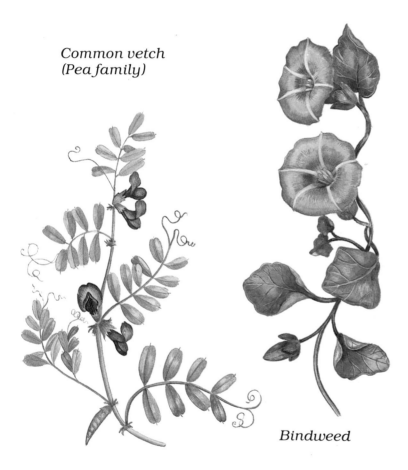

*Common vetch
(Pea family)*

Bindweed

Does bindweed twine clockwise or anti-clockwise?

There are two groups of plants called bindweed that climb up other plants by twining around their stems. One is called the Convolvulus family and they twine anti-clockwise seen from above. The other group is the Polygonum family, and they twine clockwise.

Why does moss grow in a thick mat?

Moss grows from spores. When the spore starts to grow, it sends out a thin green thread which grows branches. Buds form on the branches and grow into new moss plants. The young plants therefore grow very close together and soon form a mat. Moss leaves are not waterproof, and by growing in thick mats they keep moisture around themselves.

How do ferns grow?

Ferns do not have flowers, so they cannot produce seeds. Instead they have spores on the underside of the leaves. The spores fall to the ground and grow into little discs. The discs contain male and female cells, which later come together and grow into young ferns. Some ferns, like bracken, also spread from rhizomes, or underground stems.

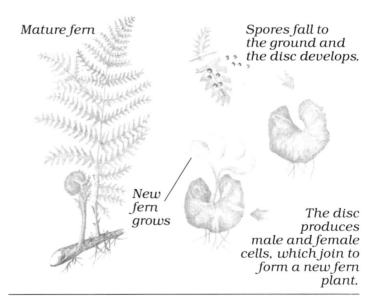

Mature fern

Spores fall to the ground and the disc develops.

New fern grows

The disc produces male and female cells, which join to form a new fern plant.

Does mistletoe ever grow on the ground?

No. Mistletoe is a parasite which lives on the branches of other trees.

How many spores can a giant puff-ball produce?

A puff-ball is a round fungus. An average-sized giant puff-ball (about the size of a football) produces about 7 million million spores. Most of them do not grow into new giant puff-balls.

Plant Names

What is the difference between annual, biennial and perennial plants?

An annual plant grows from a seed, flowers, fruits and dies all in one year. A biennial plant grows from the seed one year, and flowers, fruits and dies the next year. A perennial plant grows up, flowers and fruits from year to year.

Petunias
(Annual)

Forget-me-nots
(Biennial)

Phlox
(Perennial)

Which plant is named after the Persian word for turban?

The tulip is named after the Persian word for a turban. People thought that the flower looked like a turban, which is a head-dress made from cloth.

Why is common cat's-tail grass also called timothy-grass?

About 100 years ago an American called Timothy Hanson took some common cat's-tail grass seed from New York State to Carolina. He planted the seed to grow the grass as cattle feed, and it became known as timothy-grass after him.

Why is bedstraw so called?

Bedstraw got its name because it was once used to stuff pillows and mattresses for beds. It has thin, trailing stems with very small leaves and flowers. When dry it is rather like fine straw.

Birdsfoot trefoil

Why is birdsfoot trefoil so called?

Birdsfoot trefoil is a clover. It gets its name because the seed-pods look like the claw of a bird. The word trefoil comes from Latin words meaning 'three' and 'leaf'. Like all clovers, the leaves of birdsfoot trefoil are made of three leaflets. Clovers with four or even more leaflets are sometimes found.

What is beechmast?

The triangular brown nuts of the beech tree are sometimes called beechmast when they are lying on the ground. Beechmast is a useful source of food for animals during the winter. Great tits, for example, may depend on it.

What is belladonna?

Belladonna is another name for the very poisonous plant known as deadly nightshade. Belladonna means 'beautiful lady' in Italian, and it was probably given this name because it contains the drug atropine. If atropine is squeezed into the eye, it makes the pupil larger. At one time, ladies used it because they thought it made their eyes beautiful. Nowadays only doctors use it because it makes it easier to examine the eye.

How does bracket fungus get its name?

Bracket fungus is a kind of fungus that grows on living and dead trees. It gets its name because it grows rather like a bracket or shelf.

How did the dandelion get its name?

The name dandelion comes from three French words, *dent de lion*, which mean 'tooth of the lion'. It got this strange name because the outline of the leaves was thought to look like lion's teeth.

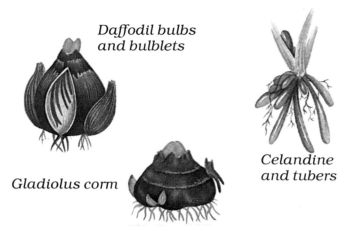

Daffodil bulbs and bulblets

Gladiolus corm

Celandine and tubers

What is the difference between a bulb, a corm and a tuber?

You can grow plants by planting bulbs, corms and tubers in the ground instead of seeds. They are parts of the plant that form underground, and they store food for the new plant that will grow up. A bulb is an underground stem and leaves, a corm is an underground stem, and a tuber is an underground stem or a root. An onion is in fact a bulb of the onion plant, and a potato is a tuber of the potato plant.

Fly agaric

Why is the fly or bug agaric toadstool so named?

The fly agaric or bug agaric toadstool is very poisonous, and its juice was once used to make preparations for killing flies or bugs. The second part of its name, agaric, comes from a Greek word meaning a kind of fungus.

Why should you avoid a destroying angel?

Because it is a deadly poisonous toadstool. It is a close relation of the death cap or death cup which can also be called the destroying angel.

Why is a spindle tree so named?

The spindle tree grows in Europe and North America where it is sometimes called the wahoo. The wood of this tree used to be used to make spindles. The spindle was used to wind wool which was spun by hand. This method of spinning is still used in some parts of the world.

Spindle tree

Flowers

Do we eat any flowers?

Yes, although we may not always realize that they are flowers. Cauliflower and broccoli are both the flower heads of kinds of cabbage. The flowers of some plants are used to make drinks. Jasmine flowers are sometimes mixed with tea to give it flavour. The flowers of many wild plants are used to make wine. Some flowers, such as violets and roses, are crystallized (cooked with sugar) to make cake decorations. Cloves, which are used for flavouring food, are the dried flower buds of an East Indian shrub. Capers, which are often pickled in vinegar, are the flower buds of a Mediterranean shrub. Some people like to eat the flowers of marrows and nasturtiums.

How are onions and lilies alike?

Lilies, onions, chives, garlic and bluebells all belong to a family of plants called the Liliaceae, or lily family. It is a very useful family. Some of the plants can be eaten, like onions, chives, leeks and garlic. Many of them have very pretty flowers which people like to grow in their gardens.

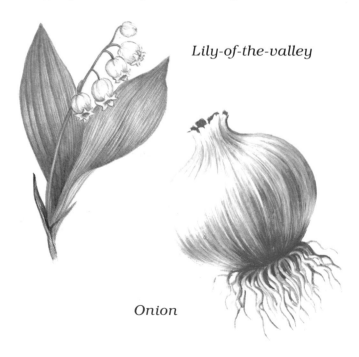

Lily-of-the-valley

Onion

What were the heads of teasels once used for?

They were used for combing out wool and for brushing cloth to give it a slightly fluffy surface. The flowering head of the teasel has many stiff bristles between the flowers. The bristles have tiny hooks on them. The heads were fixed in a wooden frame and pulled across the wool or cloth so that the bristles would catch in it. Occasionally teasels are still used in this way. Teasel comes from a word which means 'to pull about'.

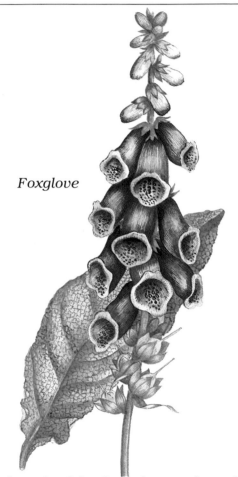

Foxglove

Which valuable drug is produced by the foxglove?

The leaves of the foxglove contain a drug called digitalis. Digitalis is used in the treatment of heart disease. It slows down the speed at which a person's heart is beating. It also helps the muscles in the heart to work better. Digitalis is obtained from the dried leaves of foxgloves. It has been used for hundreds of years and is still a very important drug for treating heart disease.

Why might balsam be described as impatient?

Most balsams belong to a group of plants called by the Latin name *Impatiens*, which means 'impatient'. This is because of the 'impatient' way in which their seed pods explode when they are touched. Balsams grow in damp places in many parts of the world and they may have yellow, orange or pink flowers.

Why are flowers coloured?

Many flowers have brightly coloured petals to attract insects. Most flowering plants rely on insects to carry pollen from flower to flower. Plants that flower at night often have pale-coloured flowers so that they show up in the dark and the night-flying moths can see them. Many flowers give off scent to attract insects to pollinate them.

Cowslip

Which pretty wild flower has a name meaning 'cow dung'?

This flower is the cowslip, which is from the old English word for cow dung. It got its name because the flowers grow in bright yellow clumps in fields, scattered like patches of cow dung.

Do all flowers have petals?

No. Some plants are pollinated by the wind or by water. They do not need to attract insects and so their flowers often do not have petals. Many of these plants bloom in early spring, so that leaves do not get in the way of the wind blowing through the branches. The catkin flower of the hazel does not have petals nor does the giant *Rafflesia*.

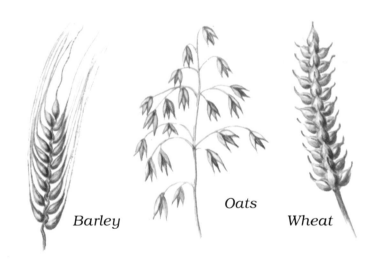

Barley   *Oats*   *Wheat*

Does grass have flowers?

Grass plants do have flowers, but they are not brightly coloured because they do not need to attract insects to pollinate them. The flowers do not have petals and when the pollen is ready it is just blown away by the wind. Grasses, such as wheat, oats and barley, are the most important source of food for people. The first farmers found that wild grass seeds scattered as easily as the pollen. Modern farmers have managed to grow crops with tighter flowering heads so that the seeds, or grain, do not fall out.

Do all flowers close at night?

Many, but not all, flowers close up at night or when the weather is cold. The daisy closes its flowers when the light begins to fade in the evening. Crocuses are even more sensitive, and will open when the sun is shining and close when it goes behind a cloud. Wood sorrel even closes its leaves at night. Some flowers, like the evening primrose, close their petals during the day and open them at night.

Trees

Spruce cones

Why do trees have bark?

The bark of a tree is like a blanket that protects the living wood inside. It stops the tree from losing too much water. It also stops too many insects and parasites from attacking the wood. The bark also helps to protect the tree from very cold or very hot weather. Bark is actually made up of two layers. The inside layer is a soft, living cork-like material. The outer layer, which you can see, is a hard, dead shell.

Why do some trees produce sticky gum or resin?

The sticky gum or resin produced by many trees helps to protect the tree from attacks by insects. It also seals any wounds in the bark such as those caused when a branch is torn off.

What is a conifer?

A tree is called a conifer if it produces its seeds in cones and has needle-like or scale-like leaves. Conifers are almost always evergreen trees. They lose, and replace, their leaves periodically but never all at the same time.

What are deciduous trees?

Deciduous trees are trees which lose their leaves in the autumn. Evergreen trees, such as most conifers, keep their leaves all year round. Deciduous trees are also called broad-leaved trees because their leaves are broader than those of conifers. All deciduous trees have flowers, although the flowers are not always obvious.

What is a pollarded tree?

If the top of a young deciduous tree is cut off about 2 metres from the ground, it will send out fresh shoots from the new top. This is called pollarding. Pollarding is done to garden trees to improve their appearance. Willows may be pollarded to encourage the growth of suitable branches for basket-making.

Beech

Common Oak

Ash

Elm

What kind of tree is used for making baskets?

Many baskets are made from the thin branches of the willow or osier. The bark is taken off to give white wood, or the branches may be boiled with the bark on, which dyes the wood. The branches are soaked so that they will bend easily for weaving into baskets. When they dry, they become firm but are still pliable, so that they do not easily break. Willow wood has many other uses because it is both light and strong.

White willow

Willow basket

Why do conifers have needle-like leaves?

The leaves of conifers are usually thin and needle-like, and are very tough, so that they do not lose much water. This allows the tree to grow in places where there is not very much water, at least for part of the year. Conifers grow in the very cold parts of the world and high up mountains, where the ground is frozen in the winter. They also grow in places where there is a fairly wet winter but a hot, dry summer, like the Mediterranean area of Europe.

How can you tell how old a tree is?

If you look at a tree stump or a cut log, you will see that it is made up of rings of different coloured wood. If you count the rings, you can tell how old the tree is in years. This is because a layer of new wood grows just beneath the bark every year. When the trunk or a branch is cut, the layers show up as rings.

Section through a tree trunk showing rings

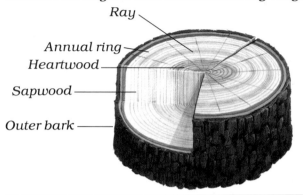

Ray

Annual ring

Heartwood

Sapwood

Outer bark

Why should cattle not graze near yew trees?

Farmers stop cattle, horses and sheep from grazing under yew trees because their leaves, bark and fruit are poisonous. The animals do not try to graze on the yew trees themselves, which they somehow know are poisonous. But they will eat pieces that have fallen off the trees or have been cut from them, and may be poisoned in this way.

Yew tree

How does a banyan tree grow so big?

A banyan tree is a kind of fig tree that grows in India and Sri Lanka. It is possible for one banyan tree to be the size of a small wood. There is a tree in Sri Lanka which is said to have 350 large trunks and more than 3000 smaller ones! The seeds of banyan trees are often dropped into the tops of other trees by birds. As the seeds start to grow, they send roots down through the air to the ground. Branches start to develop, and supports grow down from them. These supports take root as soon as they reach the ground. The supports grow into new trunks and send out more branches. These branches send down more supports and so on. After a while the tree that first supported the banyan will die.

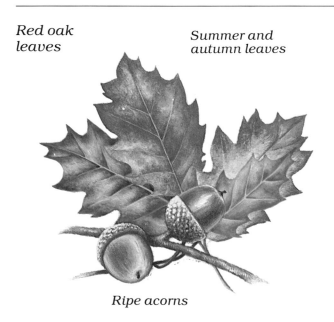

Red oak leaves

Summer and autumn leaves

Ripe acorns

Why do leaves turn yellow, red and brown in autumn?

During the summer the leaves of a tree are busy making food for the tree. They contain chlorophyll which makes them green. When autumn comes, the stalks of the leaves are sealed off and the chlorophyll decays. The leaves lose their green colour and turn yellow, red or brown before they fall off. Once the leaves have fallen, the tree rests until the following spring, using food stored during the summer. Some trees do not lose their leaves, and these are called evergreens. Most trees that have cones (conifers) are evergreen.

What is an arboretum?

An arboretum is a collection of living trees, just as a zoo is a collection of living animals. The collection has been planted and looked after to show many different kinds of trees. Such collections give people the chance to study different trees easily without having to travel to find them.

Palm tree

How is a palm different from most other trees?

Palms are unlike most other trees because they do not grow side branches. They do not grow thicker, but only taller. A pattern of scars may be seen all the way up the trunk of a palm tree. The scars mark the places where old leaves once grew. New leaves grow in a cluster at the top of the trunk. If this cluster is cut off, no more new leaves can grow, and the palm will die. The trunk of a palm tree does not have rings.

What is a bonsai?

A bonsai is a tree in a pot like a plant. It is specially cultivated so that it is a perfect miniature of a full-size tree. Most bonsai come from Japan.

Plant Records

Rafflesia

Which plant has the largest flower?

The largest flower is that of a strange plant called *Rafflesia*, or stinking corpse lily, which grows in jungles in Asia. The flowers are orangey-brown with white splotches, and measure up to 91 centimetres across. The plant in fact consists only of this large flower, and has no stem or leaves. The flowers attach themselves to vines and feed from them.

Which plant has the largest fruit?

The jackfruit, which grows in India and Sri Lanka, probably has the largest of all fruits. One fruit may be as heavy as 25 kilograms. It is an oval, yellow, spiny fruit with a sweet or sour brown pulp inside. The pulp can be eaten raw or it can be cooked in different ways.

Which plant has the largest leaves?

The raffia palm of Madagascar has the largest leaves. They can be as long as 12.2 metres. The fibre from the leaves is used for making baskets and mats and for tying plants.

What is the largest tree?

The largest tree in the world is a California big tree or giant sequoia. It grows in the Sequoia National Park in California in the United States. This tree is also the world's largest living thing. It is 83 metres tall and measures 34.9 metres round. The tree contains about 2500 tonnes of wood, and is believed to be almost 4000 years old.

Which tree lives the longest?

The bristlecone pine trees of Nevada, California and Arizona in the United States, are believed to be the oldest trees in the world. The oldest known one that is still living is about 4600 years old. It had been growing for more than 2000 years when Jesus Christ was born.

Death cap toadstool

Which is the most poisonous fungus?

The death cap or death cup toadstool is probably the most poisonous fungus in the world. Even a very small piece of it can kill, and it is particularly dangerous because the poison is not destroyed by cooking. People do not start to feel ill until about ten hours after they have eaten it. Nothing can be done to help, because there is no cure for the poison. The death cap is poisonous to all animals.

SCIENCE

How much can a microscope magnify?

An optical microscope, which uses light rays, can magnify things up to about 2500 times. An electron microscope, which uses rays of electrons, can magnify as much as a million times. Some special microscopes can magnify hundreds of millions of times and detect individual atoms.

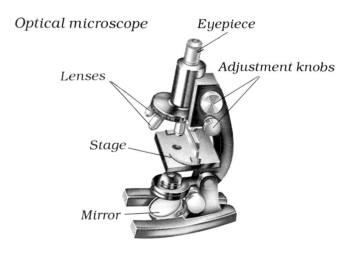

Optical microscope
Eyepiece
Lenses
Adjustment knobs
Stage
Mirror

What is the water pressure at the bottom of the sea?

The deeper you dive in the sea, the more the weight of water above presses down on you. In the deepest part of the ocean over 11 kilometres down, the water pressure is more than a tonne on every square centimetre. Yet, people in special pressurized vessels have been this deep and lived.

What is ballistics?

Ballistics is the study of the paths taken by projectiles, such as bullets and rockets.

What is absolute zero?

Absolute zero is the lowest temperature possible in theory. It is $-273.15°C$. Nothing can be colder than absolute zero. But scientists have produced temperatures only a tiny fraction of a degree above absolute zero.

Why do balloons float in the air?

Balloons can float in the air if they contain a gas that is lighter than the air. This gas is usually hydrogen or helium. Hot-air balloons are filled with air heated by a burner. They float because hot air is lighter than cold air. A balloon that you blow up with your mouth does not float but the wind may carry it aloft. The air you blow into the balloon is not lighter than the air around the balloon.

Hot-air balloons

How do we know how old rocks and remains are?

Ancient remains like bones or pots may be thousands of years old. Fossils and rocks are generally millions of years old. We can find out when they formed because everything gives out radioactive rays, though they are usually too weak to harm us. After living things die or a rock is formed, the amount of radioactivity drops steadily. By measuring the radioactivity, we can find out how old something is.

What are crystals made of?

Minerals often form in pieces that each have the same shape. These pieces are called crystals. Table salt and sugar consist of tiny crystals. Crystals are made of atoms and molecules just like everything else. They have special shapes because the atoms and molecules inside them are lined up in rows. The way in which the rows line up with each other gives a crystal its particular shape.

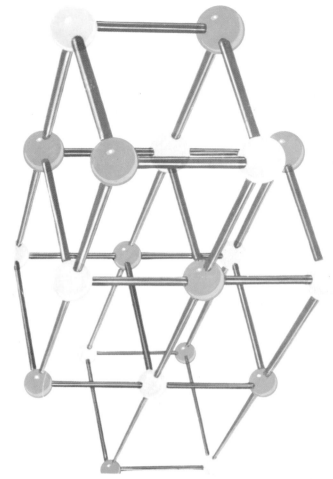

Salt crystals are made up of sodium and chlorine atoms.

What is a barometer?

A barometer is an instrument used to measure the pressure of the atmosphere.

Aneroid barometer

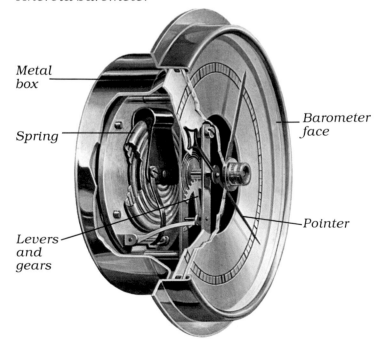

Metal box

Spring

Levers and gears

Barometer face

Pointer

What is a vacuum?

A vacuum is nothing at all. It is a space that is completely empty of air and everything else. A perfect vacuum cannot be made on Earth as it is impossible to remove everything from a container. A few molecules or atoms of air or some other substance will always remain. The best vacuum is found out in space, away from the Earth.

Is a perpetual motion machine possible?

No. Inventors have tried for centuries to build a perpetual motion machine. Such a machine would need no fuel or other supply of energy, yet would keep going for ever once you had started it. In fact, without an energy supply, every machine comes to a stop sooner or later. The moving parts rub against each other, and this friction acts like brakes to slow and then stop the machine.

Atoms and Energy

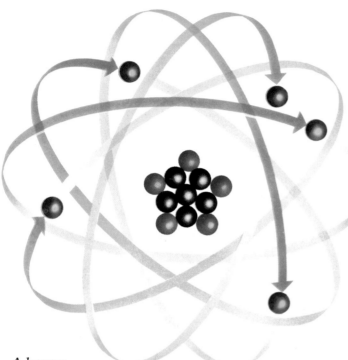

A boron atom is made up of five protons and six neutrons in the nucleus, and five electrons.

What is everything made of?

Everything is made up of tiny particles called atoms. Atoms are very small – only about a hundred-millionth of a centimetre across. There are about two million atoms in the thickness of this page. The atoms stick together tightly so that a solid object is hard. In liquids and gases, they do not stick together so tightly. In many substances, atoms form groups called molecules. The molecules all contain the same atoms arranged together in the same way.

What is inside an atom?

An atom is made up of even smaller particles. At the centre of the atom is a particle called the nucleus. It is 10,000 times smaller than the atom. Around it move even smaller particles called electrons. The electrons and the nucleus have electrical charges. These charges keep the electrons in the atom.

Who discovered atoms?

Nowadays there are special microscopes that can detect atoms. However, scientists long ago were able to work out that everything is made of atoms without having to see them. As long ago as 400 BC, the Greek philosopher Democritus said that things are made of atoms. The first scientist to work out how things contain atoms was the British chemist John Dalton. He put forward his atomic theory in 1803.

Who first split the atom?

In 1919 a New Zealand-born scientist, Ernest Rutherford, reported that he had managed to split the atom. He changed nitrogen atoms into oxygen atoms. Splitting the atom was very important, because it led the way to nuclear power.

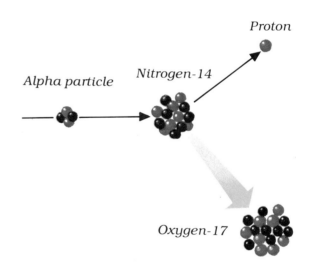

Rutherford changed nitrogen into oxygen by bombarding it with alpha particles.

Why do scientists try to smash atoms?

The nucleus of an atom, even though it is so small, is not solid. It is made of even smaller particles called protons and neutrons. And there are other tiny particles that may be found in atoms. Scientists try to break the nuclei and particles in atoms apart so that they can study these particles. They do this by bombarding them with beams of fast-moving particles. These are produced in machines called particle accelerators or atom smashers.

Why is nuclear power so very powerful?

Nuclear power, which is the same as nuclear energy or atomic energy, is the most powerful source of energy. One kilogram of nuclear fuel could produce as much energy as 3 million kilograms of coal. Nuclear fuel, such as uranium or plutonium, produces such huge amounts of energy because it loses mass or weight when it is used in a nuclear power station. This mass is turned into energy, and a little mass produces a vast amount of energy in a carefully controlled chain reaction. Atomic bombs or nuclear weapons work in the same way, but the chain reaction is uncontrolled and this is why they are so destructive.

Radioactive areas and containers are marked with the international radiation symbol.

How does a nuclear reactor work?

A nuclear reactor is the heart of a nuclear power station. In the reactor, uranium fuel produces vast amounts of heat. This heat is used to boil water to make steam. The steam goes to electricity generators to produce electricity. The uranium fuel is bombarded with particles called neutrons in the reactor. This breaks apart the nuclei in the uranium atoms, changing them into smaller nuclei. Splitting the uranium atoms produces great amounts of heat.

Why is radioactivity so dangerous?

When an atom splits to release nuclear energy, it gives out dangerous rays called radioactivity or radiation. Radiation is invisible and you cannot feel it. If you received a lot of radiation, you would become very ill and you could die. Nuclear weapons produce radiation, and this is why they are so much more dangerous than ordinary weapons. The reactors in nuclear power stations have shields to stop radioactivity getting out. But the waste material from the reactors is very radioactive, and has to be stored for safety.

Who first produced nuclear energy?

The great Italian physicist Enrico Fermi showed how nuclear power could be controlled. He built the first nuclear reactor at Chicago, USA, and it first produced energy in December 1942 by controlling a chain reaction in uranium.

When did the first nuclear weapon explode?

The first nuclear weapon exploded on 16 July 1945. It exploded in a test carried out in the United States. Two bombs were dropped on Japanese cities, Hiroshima and Nagasaki, by the United States in August 1945. They killed more than 200,000 people. No nuclear weapons have been used against people since then. There are now enough nuclear weapons to kill everyone on Earth.

The atomic bomb destroyed Hiroshima.

Light and Colour

How fast does light move?

Light rays move at a speed of 299,792·5 kilometres per second. It takes light just over a second to reach us from the Moon, 8 minutes from the Sun, and $4\frac{1}{4}$ years from the nearest star. Rays such as radio waves and X-rays travel at the same speed as light. Nothing else can move so fast.

What colour is white light?

White light, such as sunlight, is a mixture of other colours. A glass prism can split up white light into these colours. They are the colours of the rainbow. This is because raindrops split up sunlight in the same way to produce a rainbow. Mixing coloured lights can give white. If you look closely at a colour television screen, you will see that white is produced by a mixture of red, green and blue dots or stripes on the screen.

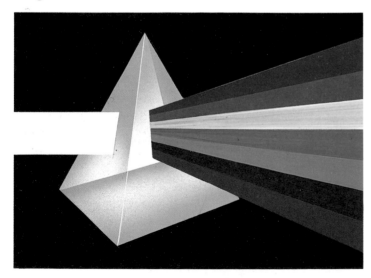

A prism splits white light into colours.

How do X-rays pass through things?

X-rays are powerful invisible rays similar to light rays. They can pass through flesh in the same way that light passes through glass. However, the rays do not pass through bones, so an X-ray photograph of the body shows up the bones inside.

What are infra-red and ultra-violet rays?

These are rays like light rays, but they are invisible to the human eye. We can feel infra-red rays, because they make us feel warm. They are in fact heat rays. Ultra-violet rays come with sunlight from the Sun. They help give us a sun tan. The rays also make luminous paints or bright fluorescent paints glow with light.

A high power laser drills a crater in stainless steel.

What is a laser?

A laser is a machine that fires a very powerful beam of light. The beam is very thin. Laser beams are used to measure distances very accurately. They have been reflected from mirrors placed on the Moon to find the exact distance of the Moon. Laser beams can be very hot, and are used to drill holes in and cut through metals and other materials. In medicine, lasers can repair damaged tissue without surgery. The name laser stands for Light Amplification by Stimulated Emission of Radiation.

Electricity

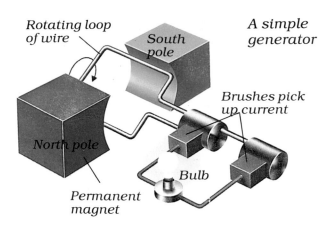

Rotating loop of wire

South pole

A simple generator

Brushes pick up current

North pole

Bulb

Permanent magnet

What is electricity?

Electricity is a form of energy. It is produced by a movement or flow of electrons. Electrons are the tiny particles in atoms. The electron movement produces an electric charge that can give energy. The energy release may be huge, as in a flash of lightning, or small, as in the glow of a torch.

Who invented the battery?

An Italian scientist called Alessandro Volta invented the battery in 1800. He was the first person to make current electricity.

Alessandro Volta's battery

How many kinds of electricity are there?

There are two kinds of electricity: static electricity and current electricity. Static electricity is a kind of electricity that does not move. It builds up on an object. Static electricity builds up in thunder clouds and causes lightning. Rubbing certain objects can produce static electricity powerful enough to make small sparks. Current electricity is a flow of electricity along a wire.

What makes electricity?

Electricity is made by batteries and electric generators. Inside a battery, there are special chemicals. The chemicals change into other chemicals and produce an electric current as they do so. The battery will work until all the chemicals have changed. An electric generator has to be powered to produce an electric current. It contains magnets and coils of wire that turn and give out electricity.

What are volts, amps, ohms and watts?

These are all units of electricity. The number of volts, or voltage, is a measure of the strength of the electricity. Batteries are marked with the voltage that they produce. The number of amps or amperes measures the amount of electric current that flows through a wire. Just how much current flows depends on the resistance of the wire, which is measured in ohms. If the resistance is low, a large current flows. The number of watts measures how much energy is produced when an electric current is used. Light bulbs are marked in watts to show how much light energy they give.

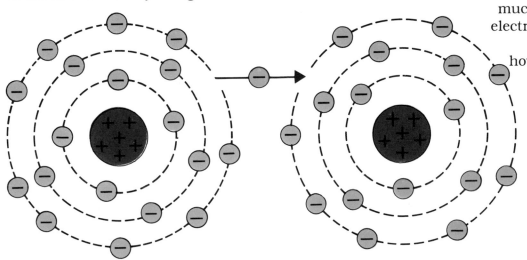

Electrons jump from one atom to the next causing electricity to flow along a wire.

Solids, Liquids and Gases

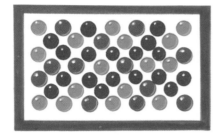

Solid

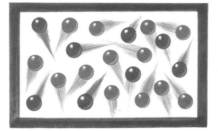

Liquid

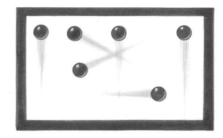

Gas

Why are some things solid and others liquid or gaseous?

Almost everything can in fact be a solid, a liquid or a gas – depending on how hot or cold it is. When they are heated, solids melt and become liquids, and liquids boil and become gases. When they are cooled, gases condense and become liquids, and liquids freeze and become solids. Solids, liquids and gases are different because their atoms or molecules are arranged differently. In solids, they are bound tightly together, making the solid hard. In liquids, the bonds between the atoms or molecules are looser so they can move easily – this enables liquids to flow. In gases, the bonds are very weak and the atoms and molecules can move apart, making gases light and thin.

What is water made of?

Water is a compound consisting of hydrogen and oxygen. In every molecule, it has twice as many hydrogen atoms as oxygen atoms and its chemical formula is H_2O.

Why does water boil?

The water in a kettle boils when its temperature reaches boiling point, which is 100°C. The water molecules move faster and faster as the water gets hotter. At boiling point, the molecules become free of each other. The liquid water turns into gaseous water, or steam. The steam rises from the water in the kettle, and mingles with the air.

Why does water freeze?

In water, the water molecules move about though they are still bound loosely together. As the water cools, the molecules slow down and the bonds between them get stronger. As the water reaches freezing point − 0°C, the molecules become firmly bound together, and the water becomes hard and solid as ice forms.

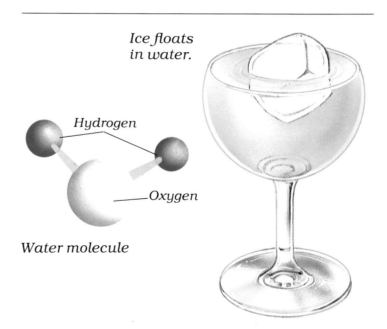

Ice floats in water.

Hydrogen

Oxygen

Water molecule

Why does ice float in water?

It seems odd that water should freeze into a solid that is lighter or less dense than water so that it floats. The reason is that, as the water molecules become bound together on freezing, they move apart slightly. The ice expands in size as it forms, making it lighter than the water that is freezing.

Elements and Metals

Gold bars and nuggets

What is an element?

An element is a substance made up of exactly similar atoms. More than 100 elements are known.

Which element is most abundant?

In the whole Universe, there is more hydrogen than any other element. This is because stars are made of hydrogen. On Earth, the most abundant element is oxygen.

Which element was first discovered in the Sun?

Helium was discovered in 1868 by studying the light from the Sun. A little helium is produced by minerals, but it was not discovered on Earth until 1895.

Which metal is a liquid?

We think of metals as being hard and solid, but one metal is usually a liquid. This is the metal mercury, which is silver in colour. Some thermometers contain mercury. In fact, you can make any metal liquid if you heat it so much that it melts. Mercury becomes solid if it is cooled to −39°C.

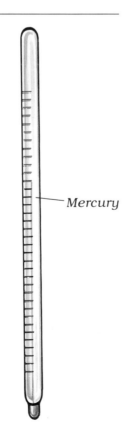

— *Mercury*

The mercury inside a thermometer rises as the temperature goes up and falls as the temperature drops.

Why are gold and silver precious metals?

Gold and silver are precious because they look attractive, and beautiful jewellery and other objects can be made from them. They are also valuable because gold and silver conduct electricity very well. They are used in making electrical equipment of the highest quality. However, the main reason why gold and silver are so costly is that both metals are rare.

Why does metal feel cold?

If you get up and touch a piece of metal in the room where you are reading this book, it will feel cold. The reason for this is that the metal takes some heat away from your fingertips, and makes them cold. It does this because a metal is a good conductor of heat, and heat moves through it easily.

Which metal is obtained from bauxite?

Bauxite is an ore from which the metal aluminium is obtained.

Which is the heaviest metal?

The heaviest metal is a rare metal called osmium. It is nearly 23 times as heavy as the same amount of water, and twice as heavy as lead. This means that a football made of osmium would weigh about 120 kilograms – probably more than twice as much as you weigh.

Materials and Machines

What is a robot?

A robot is a machine that can carry out a task on its own. Robots are designed to do a particular job over and over again. They can make metal parts or assemble cars, for example. With computers for brains, robots can perform a wide range of tasks, and make decisions on their own.

Extendible arm

Finger gripper

Control cabinet with memory store

Unimate 2000 is a heavy-duty robot.

Operator controls

How big is the brain of a calculator?

A calculator is a small computer, and it has a brain made up of thousands of electronic parts. The brain works by counting the electrical signals produced when you press the keys of the calculator. The parts do not have to be big to do this; in fact the whole brain of the calculator can be smaller than your little fingernail!

When was the computer invented?

The first electronic computer, which is the kind in use today, was built in Britain in 1943. It was called Colossus. This computer was developed in total secrecy during World War II to crack enemy codes. However, the principles of computers were worked out about a century before Colossus by the British mathematician Charles Babbage. His Analytical Engine was to have the same parts as a modern computer but in a very simple form and it was to work in a similar way. However, the Analytical Engine was never built.

How fast can computers work?

The most powerful computers can add up hundreds of millions of numbers in a second – and get the total exactly right! In a minute, computers can do calculations that would take a person a whole lifetime to complete.

How does a camera work?

When you press the shutter of a camera, it lets light through the lens for a fraction of a second. The light forms a picture on the film inside the camera. The film is coated with chemicals that change slightly when light falls on them. But to see the picture, the film has to be placed in other chemicals so that the picture develops. In some cameras, the developing chemicals are contained with the film. The photograph emerges from the camera, and the picture develops while you wait.

The largest computers are mainframe computers.

What is paper made of?

Paper is made from wood, and from other plant materials such as cotton rags. The wood and other materials are made into pulp by grinding them with water. The pulp is then spread out in layers, and the layers are dried to produce sheets of paper. The paper consists of little fibres of wood or other material all tangled up together. Substances such as glues or dyes are added to make special kinds of paper.

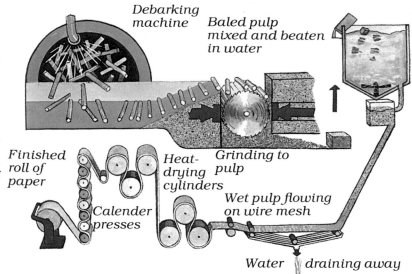

This diagram shows how paper is made from wood.

Where does sugar come from?

Sugar comes from two different plants, sugar cane and sugar beet. The sugar is in the juice of the sugar cane, and in the roots of the sugar beet. Machines crush the sugar cane to get the juice. The sugar beet roots are placed in hot water to extract the sugar from them. The sugar juice or extract is then heated to obtain the sugar.

What is glass made of?

Glass is made by heating sand, lime and soda together in a furnace. The ingredients melt, and glass is formed. Glass goes soft when it is heated, and all kinds of objects are made by shaping hot glass.

Hydrofoil

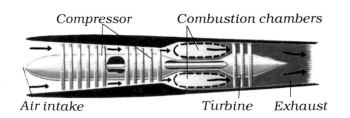

Turbojet engine

What is a hydrofoil?

A hydrofoil is a boat with wings, but the wings are underwater! The wings are like fins. As the hydrofoil picks up speed, the fins rise in the water and lift the hull clear of the surface. A long propeller drives the hydrofoil along. As the hull is out of the water, a ride in a hydrofoil is smooth and fast. It can skim through the water at speeds of up to about 160 kilometres an hour.

How does a jet engine work?

The jet engines on an aircraft have turbines that suck in air. The air is then heated by burning paraffin or kerosene. The heating makes the air expand, and it rushes out of the exhaust. As it does so, it drives another turbine connected to the first turbine. The engine's great power comes from the expansion of the air inside it. This pushes the engine forward as the air streams out of the exhaust.

When were tanks first used in war?

The first tanks were used by the British army during World War I. They went into action in France in September 1916. They could only move at walking pace, but they were a success.

The first tank was known as 'Little Willie' and had no guns.

How does radar work?

Radar shows airport controllers where aircraft are as they approach and leave the airport. In this way, they can guide the aircraft so that they take off and land safely. Radar transmitters at the airport send out radar signals. These are like radio waves, and they bounce off the aircraft and back to the transmitter. The returning radar signals go to the control tower, where they are turned into pictures and show the positions of the aircraft.

When was printing invented?

Printing began in Korea and China in about AD 700. Wooden printing blocks were used to print on scrolls. In Europe, the first books were printed by Johann Gutenberg, who lived in Germany. In about 1455, he made the first printed Bible.

Matchbox

When were matches invented?

The first matches that lit by striking them on a rough surface appeared in 1827. They were invented by a British chemist called John Walker. Walker was trying to invent an explosive material for guns. He stirred the material with a stick, and then scraped the stick on the floor to remove material from it. Instead, the material burst into flame. From this, Walker got the idea of making matches.

Which kind of clock is the most accurate?

The most accurate kind of clock is an atomic clock. Atomic clocks are not like ordinary clocks that show the time. They are used in science to measure extremely short intervals of time. If an atomic clock could continue to work for a million years, it would still be right to within a second after all this time.

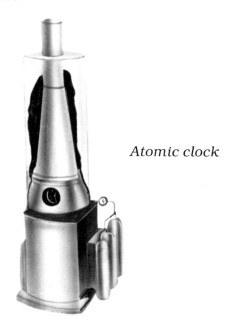

Atomic clock

What are plastics made of?

Unlike glass or paper, plastics are not directly made of natural materials. They are made from chemicals, which are obtained from oil, coal and other natural materials. By heating the chemicals so that they react in various ways, all kinds of different plastics can be made.

Building

How high is the tallest building?

The tallest building that contains floors and rooms is the Sears Tower in Chicago in the United States. It is 443 metres high – about the height of 70 two-storey houses piled on top of each other. The tower is an office building and has about 16,000 windows, one for every person who works there. The CN Tower in Toronto in Canada is higher, measuring 555 metres tall. It is a slender needle-shaped tower of solid concrete that serves as a broadcasting station for television signals. It has a restaurant over halfway up.

When were lifts or elevators first installed in buildings?

The safety lift or elevator, which does not fall if the cable breaks, was invented by the American inventor Elisha Otis. The first one to carry people was installed in a store in New York in 1857.

Where is the biggest man-made structure?

The tallest structures made by people are TV masts held up by cables. The tallest TV masts are 600 metres high. The greatest structure in volume ever built is the Great Wall of China. Its total length is about 6300 kilometres, and it is as much as 12 metres high and 10 metres wide. The Wall was constructed between 300 BC and 200 BC by an army of about 300,000 men. It was built to keep out Mongolian invaders.

Where is the longest bridge?

The longest bridge in the world crosses Lake Pontchartrain in Louisiana in the United States. It is nearly $38\frac{1}{2}$ kilometres long. The longest single span of any bridge is the main span of the Humber Estuary Bridge in England. It is 1410 metres long. An even longer span is being constructed in Japan.

The CN (Canadian National) Tower, on the shore of Lake Ontario in Toronto, is 555 metres tall.

Where is the longest tunnel?

The longest tunnel for use by people is a railway tunnel bored under the sea bed in Japan. It is 54 kilometres long. Large pipes carrying water supplies to cities may be longer than rail tunnels.

How many rooms has the world's biggest hotel?

The biggest hotel in the world is the Hotel Rossiya in Moscow in Russia. It has 3200 rooms, and 6000 people can stay there.

Transport

Who invented the helicopter?

The first helicopter to lift a person off the ground in a free flight was built by a French mechanic called Paul Cornu. In 1907, his helicopter rose 2 metres into the air with a man aboard. The first person to have the idea of the helicopter was the Italian artist Leonardo da Vinci, who lived from 1452 to 1519. He sketched a machine resembling a helicopter, and may have made a model of one.

The Montgolfier brothers' balloon

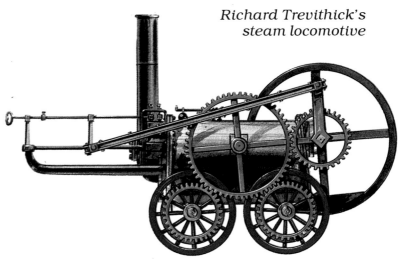

Richard Trevithick's steam locomotive

Who was the first person to fly?

The first person to go up in a balloon was the first person to fly. He was a French doctor called Pilâtre de Rozier. In October 1783, he ascended 25 metres in a hot-air balloon tethered to the ground. The balloon was made by two brothers, Joseph and Jacques Montgolfier. A month later, Pilâtre de Rozier and the Marquis d'Arlandes made the first flight in a balloon across Paris.

Who built the first petrol-driven motor car?

The first petrol-driven car was built by the German engineer Karl Benz in 1885.

First petrol-driven car

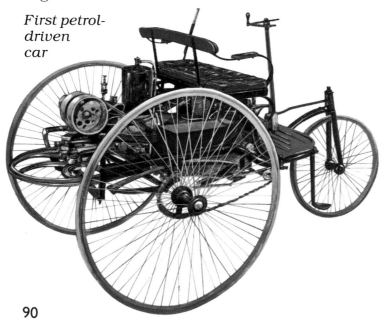

When were railways first built?

The first railway engine was built by the British engineer Richard Trevithick in 1804. His steam locomotive hauled a load of 10 tonnes of iron and 70 people along a track in Wales. The first public railway service opened in Wales in 1807, but the trains were pulled by horses at first. It was not until 1830 that steam locomotives began to pull passenger trains. The first steam services were in England, between Stockton and Darlington.

Which city had the first underground railway?

The first underground railway was built in London in 1863. The first line was called the Metropolitan Railway, and it was 6 kilometres long. Steam locomotives pulled the trains, and it must have been very smoky to travel on them. Nowadays, all underground railways have electric trains.

Flyer 1

When did the first aircraft fly?

The first machine to carry a man through the air was a glider invented by the British engineer Sir George Cayley. In 1853, he persuaded his coachman to fly the glider across a valley. The coachman made a flight of about 500 metres, becoming the first aircraft pilot in history, and promptly resigned in case Sir George asked him to do it again. The first powered aircraft was built by the American inventors Orville and Wilbur Wright. Orville made the first powered flight in 1903 at Kitty Hawk in North Carolina. The aircraft, *Flyer 1*, stayed in the air for 12 seconds and rose about 3 metres off the ground.

What is a monorail?

A monorail is a train that runs on one rail. The rail is supported above the ground. The train either hangs from wheels that run on the rail, or it runs directly on the rail, which lies beneath the centre of the train. Monorails operate in some cities instead of underground trains. They can be built above main roads, and do not take up much space.

Who invented the pneumatic tyre?

John Dunlop, a Scottish vet, invented the pneumatic (air-filled) rubber tyre for his son's tricycle in 1887.

How does an aircraft stay up in the air?

An aircraft is heavier than air, yet it manages to fly. As the wings move through the air, the air is pushed away from the top surface of the wing. There is a greater pressure of air beneath the wing than above it. As a result, air pressure acts to push the wing upwards. The wings lift and support the aircraft in the air while it is moving. To get enough lift and rise into the air, the aircraft has to speed along the ground first.

Which was the first ship to be powered by steam?

The first steamboat was a paddle steamer built by the Marquis d'Abbans. In 1783, it made a run on the River Saône in France, becoming the first vessel to move on water under its own power.

What are airships?

Airships are huge balloons with propellers to drive them, and they were once used to carry as many as 200 passengers. The airships were filled with hydrogen, a light gas. However, hydrogen is also inflammable. There were several disasters in which airships caught fire, and they disappeared by the end of the 1930s. However, airships are now flying again, but they are not common. They are lifted by helium gas, which does not catch fire.

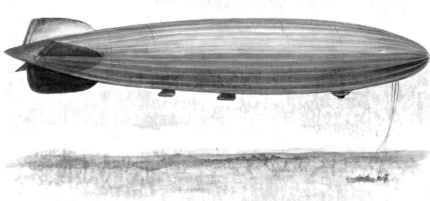

Airship

How big is the biggest aircraft?

The world's heaviest aircraft is the Antonov An-225 Myira (Dream), which weighs as much as 508 tonnes at take-off. The Boeing 747 Jumbo Jet weighs up to 395 tonnes and has carried 674 people, more than any other aircraft.

How fast is the fastest aircraft?

The fastest aircraft is a rocket-powered aircraft made in the United States. In 1967, it reached a speed of 7297 kilometres an hour. The fastest jet aircraft in the world is believed to be the Lockheed SR-71A, a military plane flown by the United States Air Force. It holds the air speed record of 3530 kilometres an hour, which it gained in 1976.

How fast can the fastest boat go?

The world water speed record is 514 kilometres an hour. This record was captured in 1978 by Kenneth Warby in a hydroplane on Blowering Dam Lake in New South Wales, Australia. However, in 1977, Kenneth Warby reached a speed of about 560 kilometres an hour, but this was not in a record attempt.

Lockheed SR-71A

Where is the biggest airport?

The airport with the biggest ground area is at Riyadh in Saudi Arabia. It covers 221 square kilometres, the size of a city. However, the world's busiest airport is at Chicago.

How fast can railway trains go?

The fastest railway trains are the TGV electric trains operated by French Railways. In 1990 a TGV reached a top speed of 515 kilometres an hour. In service, these high-speed trains carry passengers at an average speed of over 200 kilometres an hour. Magnetic levitation trains on special tracks are also very fast. An experimental magnetic levitation train in Japan has reached over 400 kilometres an hour.

The French National Railway's TGV

Where is the biggest railway station?

The biggest railway station is Grand Central Terminal in New York. It has 67 tracks, all underground. About 200,000 people arrive at or depart from Grand Central every day.

Where is the biggest seaport?

The biggest harbour in the world is at New York. Nearly 400 ships could dock there at the same time. However, the busiest port is at Rotterdam in Holland. It may handle more than 200,000 vessels a year, or one every $2\frac{1}{2}$ minutes.

What was the first jet?

The first jet-propelled aircraft was the German Heinkel He 178VI. It was built in 1939.

How fast is the fastest car?

The official world land speed record is held by a jet-engined car called *Thrust 2* which travelled at 1019 kilometres an hour across the Nevada Desert in 1983. In 1970 a rocket-engined car called the *Blue Flame* set a record of 1001 kilometres an hour. On its fastest run, the car topped 1046 kilometres an hour.

Where were the first bus services?

The first buses to carry passengers were introduced in Paris in 1662. A company to run bus services was formed by the French scientist and philosopher Blaise Pascal. The buses were horse-drawn, and carried eight passengers.

Which is the biggest ship in the world?

The world's largest ships are oil tankers. The biggest is the *Hellas Fos* of 551,000 tonnes deadweight. *Seawise Giant*, now renamed *Happy Giant*, was originally 458 metres long, 69 metres wide and 564,000 tonnes. Damaged by air attack it was made smaller during refitting work.

How slow can aircraft fly?

The slowest aircraft are helicopters, which can hover in the air without moving. Aircraft with wings have to fly above a certain speed, otherwise they will crash. However, pedal-powered aircraft can fly very slowly. In 1979, a man-powered aircraft flew across the English Channel for the first time. Its average speed was 13 kilometres an hour – no faster than you can run!

The Blue Flame

Sound and Communications

How does sound reach our ears?

Sound travels through the air to reach our ears. It will also travel through water, and through hard materials like steel and glass. This is why you can hear sounds coming from outside your home. Sound travels in waves. As you speak, you set air molecules vibrating. The movements produce sound waves that travel through the air. When the waves reach someone's ears, they set their eardrums vibrating and the person hears you speaking.

The number of sound waves a second is called the frequency of the waves. The higher the frequency, the higher the sound.

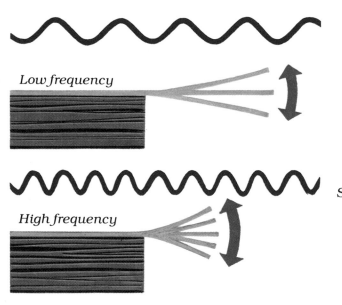

Low frequency

High frequency

What is magnetic tape used for?

Magnetic tape, like the tape in a cassette, is used to record audio or sound, especially music; video, or television pictures and sound; and the information that is fed into computers. Magnetic discs may be used instead of tape, especially in computers. To record, the sound, pictures or information are converted into electric signals, and these signals are recorded as magnetic patterns on the tape or disc. On playback, the magnetic patterns produce electric signals, from which the sound, pictures or information are obtained.

Who invented the tape recorder?

The forerunner of the tape recorder was invented by a Dane, Valdemar Poulsen, in 1899.

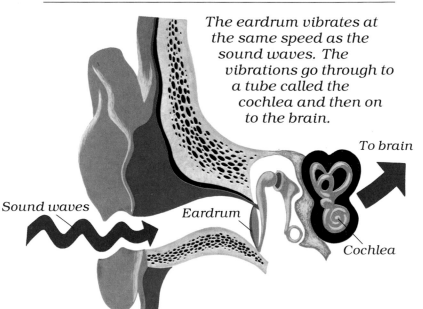

The eardrum vibrates at the same speed as the sound waves. The vibrations go through to a tube called the cochlea and then on to the brain.

To brain

Sound waves

Eardrum

Cochlea

What are ultrasonic sounds?

Even if you have the very best hearing, there are sounds that you cannot hear. They are called ultrasonic sounds, and they are too high in pitch for us to detect. Bats produce ultrasonic sounds to guide themselves through the dark. Engineers use ultrasonic sounds to examine objects and make sure there are no flaws inside them. Doctors are able to 'look' at a baby before it is born by examining its mother with ultrasonic detectors.

How does a compact disc work?

On the surface of the disc are millions of tiny holes. The holes form patterns that are code numbers. Each number is a measure of the sound. When the disc is played, the holes make a laser beam in the compact disc player flash on and off very quickly to produce light signals. A computer changes the light signals into sound. This method of recording sound is called digital recording because it uses code numbers.

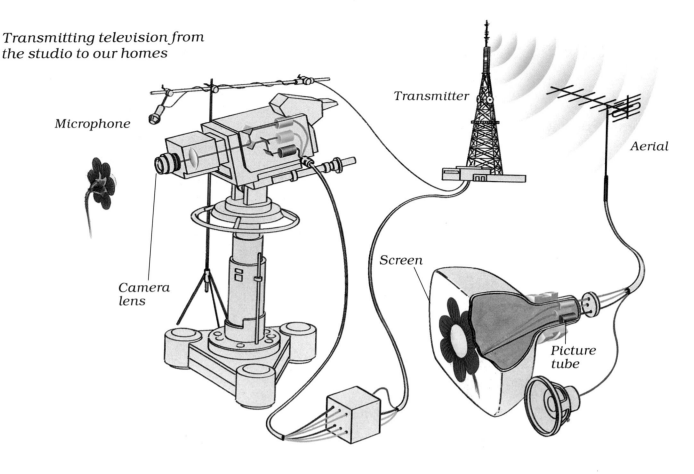

Transmitting television from the studio to our homes

Microphone

Camera lens

Transmitter

Aerial

Screen

Picture tube

Who invented radio?

The radio signals that carry radio and television programmes to your home were discovered by the German scientist Heinrich Hertz in 1887. In his honour, these signals are now measured in units called hertz. In the 1890s, the Italian engineer Guglielmo Marconi discovered how to send radio messages in the form of signals such as Morse code. In 1901, he sent a message across the Atlantic Ocean. The first radio broadcasts soon followed.

When did television services begin?

The television system now in use throughout the world uses electronic tubes to produce a picture. The first public television service using this system began in Germany in 1935. However, people did not have their own television sets, and had to go to special viewing rooms to see the programmes. The first services to enter people's homes began in Britain in 1936. There were about a hundred sets able to receive the service.

How do radio and television programmes reach our homes?

Radio and television programmes are usually transmitted from high masts some distance away. The programmes are in the form of invisible radio signals. These travel through space just as light rays do, and just as fast. The signals reach the aerial or antenna in your home and produce a weak current of electricity in it. The current flows down the cable to your radio or television set, and there it is converted into sound or pictures.

How many grooves are there on a record?

There are just two grooves on a record – one on each side. The groove is cut in a spiral in the surface of the record. For stereophonic sound, a different sound is recorded in each wall of the groove. The pick-up produces two signals, and one goes to the left-hand speaker and the other to the right-hand speaker. When you listen to the record, the sound is spread out between the two speakers.

Discoveries and Inventions

Why did Archimedes leap out of his bath?

Archimedes was the most brilliant scientist of ancient Greece. He lived in Sicily, then a Greek colony, in the 200s BC. The king asked Archimedes to find a way of making sure that his crown was made of pure gold. Archimedes worked out how to do it while in his bath. He leapt out of the bath shouting 'Eureka!', which means 'I've found it!' What Archimedes had in fact discovered was the principle which explains how objects float. He used it to test the crown, which was not pure gold. The goldsmith was later executed.

How many inventions did Thomas Edison make?

Thomas Edison was a famous American inventor. He lived from 1847 to 1931. Edison made over 1000 inventions in all. The most famous is the phonograph or gramophone, which Edison invented in 1877. Edison also invented or improved the electric light bulb, the motion picture film, the telegraph, the telephone, the electric generator and the battery.

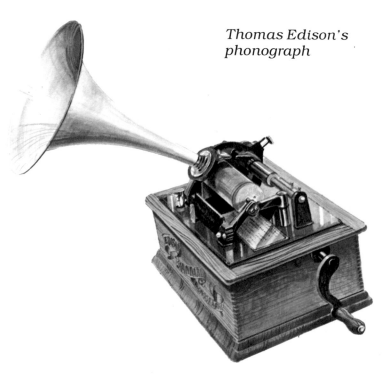

Thomas Edison's phonograph

Marie and Pierre Curie

Who was the first great woman scientist?

The first woman to make a great discovery in science was Marie Curie. She realized that new elements that are radioactive must exist. With her husband, Pierre Curie, she then discovered two of them – polonium and radium. Marie Curie lived from 1867 to 1934. She was born in Poland, but lived most of her life in France.

What is the theory of relativity?

The theory of relativity is one of the most important theories ever stated. It explains, among other things, why nuclear energy is so powerful, and how stars exist in space. It was proposed by Albert Einstein, who was born in Germany in 1879 and died in the United States in 1955. Einstein was not very good at school, but he became one of the greatest scientists who ever lived.

Who flew a kite in a thunderstorm?

In 1752, the American scientist Benjamin Franklin carried out one of the most dangerous experiments ever performed. To find out if there is electricity in thunder clouds, he flew a kite in a thunderstorm. The kite picked up electricity from the clouds. This showed that lightning is a giant electrical spark in the sky.

Alexander Graham Bell and his telephone, 1892

Who invented the telephone?

The telephone was invented by the inventor Alexander Graham Bell in America in 1875. He was working on a device to transmit sound over wires. One day he called for his assistant, who was in another room, saying 'Mr Watson, please come here. I want you.' The assistant heard Bell's voice coming from the device. This was the first telephone call.

Who made a famous discovery by watching an apple fall?

One of the greatest scientists ever to have lived was the English scientist Sir Isaac Newton. He lived from 1642 to 1727, and made many important discoveries. When Newton was a young man, he watched an apple fall from a tree. He wondered if the force that made the apple fall also kept the Moon and planets in their orbits. This force is called gravity. Newton was right, but he was unable to prove it until nearly twenty years later.

Who took the first photograph?

Joseph Niepce, a French inventor, took the first photograph in 1826. It was a view from the window of his house, and the exposure took eight hours.

Why can you see yourself in a mirror?

You can see everything around you because light rays come from everything to your eyes. You can see yourself in a mirror because light rays from your body bounce off the mirror and come back to your eyes. You can see your reflection in a glass window and in water for the same reason. The reflections are not so bright because some light rays go into the glass or water instead of bouncing back.

Who invented braille?

Braille is a system of writing for the blind that uses characters made up of raised dots. It is read using the sense of touch. A Frenchman, Louis Braille, invented it in 1829.

Who invented the steam engine?

Several people made inventions that developed the steam engine. The most important was James Watt, a Scottish engineer who lived from 1736 to 1819. Watt's steam engine was the first powerful engine, and it brought about the development of industry in mills and factories throughout Britain. James Watt is supposed to have been inspired by watching a kettle boil. He noticed that the power of the steam could lift the lid of the kettle.

James Watt's steam engine, 1788

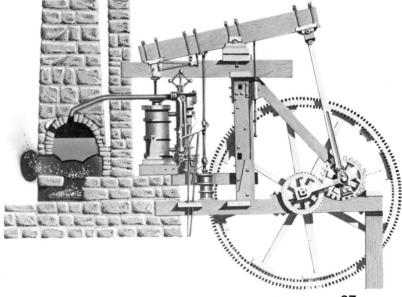

HUMAN BODY

How many cells are there in your body?

All living things are made up of cells. The simplest consist of only one cell, but your body contains millions and millions of cells. Each part of the body is made up of its own kind of cells. There are bone cells, brain cells, blood cells and so on. The smallest cells are red blood cells, which are less than a thousandth of a centimetre across. The largest cells are nerve cells that may be about a metre long but very thin.

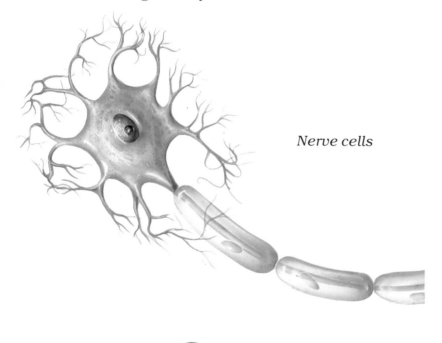

Nerve cells

Red blood cells

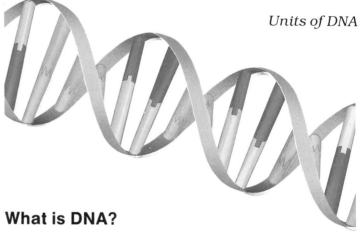

Units of DNA

What is DNA?

DNA stands for deoxyribonucleic acid. This is a substance that is present in every living cell. However, each living thing has a different kind of DNA. The kind of DNA you have in your cells gives you all the features you inherit from your parents.

How many bones are there in your body?

There are 206 main bones in the human body, plus a few small bones called sesamoid bones that vary in number. Some people may have more because they have extra ribs, and others may have fewer because some of the bones may be joined together.

What is your most important bone?

The most important bone is your backbone, which is the bone in your neck and down your back, where it is called the spine. The whole backbone is made up of 33 separate bones called vertebrae, so it can bend easily. Most bones will mend if you break them, but if you break your backbone, you may die.

Where are your humerus, radius and ulna?

These are the names of the bones in your arms. The humerus is the upper arm bone, above the elbow. Beneath the elbow, your arm bone splits in two. One bone is called the radius, and the other the ulna.

Where are your tibia, fibula and femur?

These are the names of the bones in your legs. The femur is the upper leg bone or thigh bone, above the knee. It is the longest bone in your body. Beneath the knee, you have two leg bones. At the front is the tibia or shin bone. To one side is the fibula.

Where is your sternum?

Your sternum is not at your stern, as you might think. It is in fact in front of you. It is the medical name for your breastbone, which is the flat bone you can feel in the middle of your chest.

How many ribs do you have?

Your ribs form a cage that protects your heart and lungs. You can feel them in your chest and around your back. The ribs extend in pairs from your spine, and most join at the front to your sternum (breastbone) in the centre of your chest. You should have twelve pairs of ribs in all, though some people have an extra pair. The extra ribs do not do any harm.

Why do we get goose pimples?

Your skin goes pimply if you get cold. The little pimples are called goose pimples, because they make the skin look like that of a plucked goose. Americans call them goose bumps. What happens is that little muscles in the skin raise the hairs on your skin, producing little bumps or pimples. Your skin does this to try and thicken your covering of hair to keep you warm.

Why do people have skins of different colours?

People's skins vary in colour greatly. Light-coloured people come from northern regions and dark-skinned people from the warmer parts of the world. In the East, there are people whose skins are slightly yellow in colour. Because people have travelled a lot, different skin colours can be seen almost everywhere. The differences in colour may have arisen because a dark skin gives more protection against burning by sunlight. Therefore, the people in sunny countries became darker than those in cold countries. People inherit their skin colour from their parents, so it does not change if they go and live in warmer or colder places.

Human skeleton

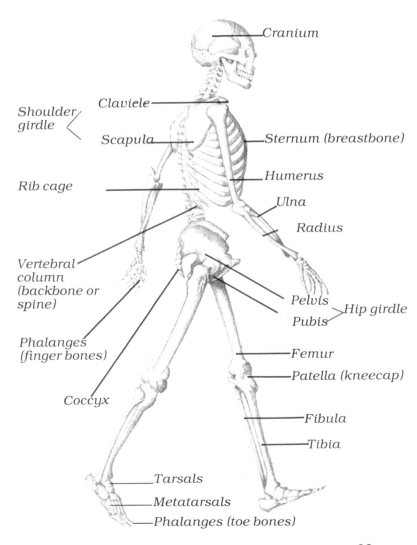

How fast do nails grow?

Nails grow at a rate of about $2\frac{1}{2}$ to 5 centimetres a year. With cutting, your fingernails and toenails replace themselves about once every six months. However, the nails will keep on growing if you do not cut them. They could get as long as 60 centimetres. The nails curl as they get very long, making it difficult to handle things.

Fingernail

Half moon

Cuticle

What is a bruise?

You get a bruise on your skin if something hits you hard. You get a red patch that goes a dark blue colour and is painful. What happens is that a little blood escapes below the skin, and then darkens in colour. A bruise is not harmful unless it is very severe. It should soon fade and disappear.

Why can a cold key or ice on the back of your neck stop a nosebleed?

It is sometimes possible to stop a nosebleed by placing a cold key or some ice on your neck, as well as over the nose itself. The sudden cold helps to close the little arteries that carry blood to the nose, thus stopping the bleeding.

What are freckles?

Freckles are little spots of colour in the skin. They show up when the skin is exposed to the sun because they are tiny patches of skin that tan more quickly than the surrounding skin.

How fast does hair grow?

Your hair grows at the rate of about 15 centimetres a year. If you do not cut your hair, it usually grows to about your waist but not much longer. The hairs on your head still keep on growing, but when each single hair gets to about this length, it drops out. A new hair then begins to grow from your head in its place.

Why does hair turn grey and white as people grow older?

Your hair is coloured because it contains a pigment called melanin. The hair is light or dark depending on the amount of melanin in it. As people grow older, the supply of melanin may stop. The hairs still grow, but they are grey or white instead of their original colour.

Why do some people have straight hair and others have curly hair?

There are between 100,000 and 200,000 hairs on your head, and they grow out of tiny holes in your skin called follicles. As a hair grows, it squeezes through the follicle rather like toothpaste being squeezed from a tube. The shape of the follicle makes the hair straight, wavy or curly. Round follicles produce straight hair, oval follicles give wavy hair and square follicles make hair that is curly.

Straight, wavy and curly hairs grow from follicles of different shapes.

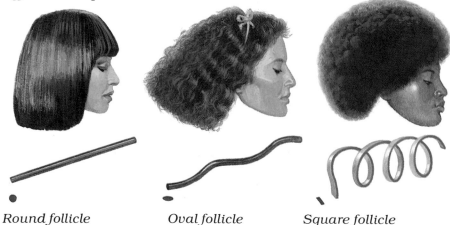

Round follicle　　　*Oval follicle*　　　*Square follicle*

How much blood is there in your body?

The amount of blood you have depends on how much you weigh. A fully-grown person has about 5 litres of blood, but a child has less.

What happens when a scab forms?

If you cut or scratch yourself, a scab soon forms over the damaged skin. It is made of dried blood and other substances. The scab is a shield that prevents germs from entering the damaged skin. Beneath the scab, the skin mends. The scab will drop off when it is no longer needed.

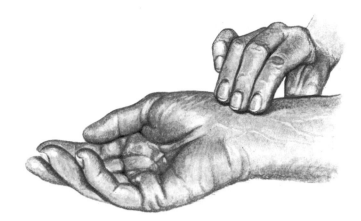

How to feel your pulse

How a wound heals

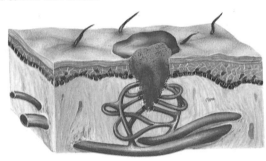

1. Blood flowing through the wound thickens and clots, forming a web which traps blood cells.

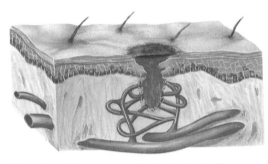

2. The blood cells dry and shrink to form a scab.

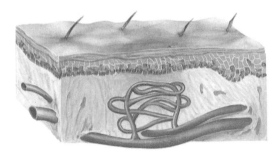

3. New skin grows beneath the scab, and when this skin is fully formed, the scab falls off.

How can you measure your heartbeat?

You can measure your heartbeat or pulse by feeling for the regular throb in your wrist, and counting the number of throbs in a minute. What you are feeling are waves of blood travelling from the heart through the artery in the wrist.

How fast does your heart beat?

In most people, the heart beats at about the rate of 70 beats every minute. However, you can have a normal heartbeat or pulse of as little as 50 beats or as many as 100 beats a minute without anything being wrong with you. During your whole life, your heart will probably beat about 3000 million times!

Does an adult's heart beat faster or slower than a child's heart?

As a person gets older, their heartbeat slows down. By the time a person reaches old age, their heart may be beating at half the rate it was when they were born.

Where is your cranium?

Your cranium is the part of your skull that encloses the brain. It is made of bone about half a centimetre thick.

How long does a baby grow inside its mother?

A baby takes 38 weeks (about 9 months) to grow inside its mother before it is born. The baby begins to grow when a sperm from the father meets the ovum (egg) in her womb. It grows until its body is fully-formed, and then the baby is ready to be born. It may stay in the womb a little longer, and babies can be born before or after 9 months without any danger.

How a baby grows

Sperm cell *Ovum*

1. The egg cell is fertilized.

2. The fertilized egg divides into two.

3. Division continues until a ball of cells forms and settles in the womb.

4. After 5 weeks the embryo (the name for the baby at this stage) is about 10mm long.

Umbilical cord

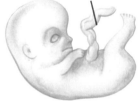

5. By 8 weeks the foetus (the name for the baby at this stage) is about 40mm long. The umbilical cord joins the baby to its mother through a special organ called the placenta.

Placenta

Amniotic fluid

Umbilical cord

6. By 38 weeks (9 months), the baby has taken up its 'birth' position head down in the womb. It is about 43cm long.

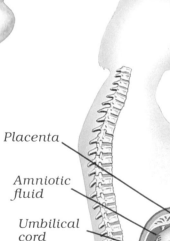

What is the first thing a newborn baby does?

A new baby has to breathe for itself so it cries to start breathing.

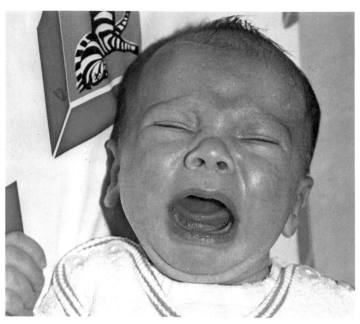

A newborn baby

How much do newborn babies sleep?

Newborn babies sleep nearly all the time – about 18 to 20 hours a day. They wake up every 2 or 3 hours when they are hungry.

Can newborn babies see?

A newborn baby cannot focus its eyes to see clearly but it can tell the difference between light and darkness.

After about 3 months a new baby can recognize its parents' faces.

Can identical twins be different sexes?

No. All identical twins, who look exactly alike, are either both boys or both girls. They cannot be a boy and a girl. Non-identical twins, who look different from each other, may be either both boys, both girls, or a boy and a girl. Triplets and quadruplets may be identical or non-identical, like twins. But the identical children are always of the same sex, as with twins.

Identical twins

What is a test-tube baby?

A test-tube baby is no different from any other baby. But, instead of beginning to grow inside its mother's womb, it begins outside her body in a special machine. An ovum (egg) is taken from the mother and fertilized with the father's sperm in the machine (which is called a test-tube, but isn't really). Then the egg is put back in the mother's womb, and it grows normally. Eventually, a healthy normal baby is born. The mother is treated in this way if she cannot otherwise have children.

How many babies can be born together?

Usually, a mother has just one baby. Sometimes, she has twins (two babies), or triplets (three) or even quadruplets (four). The babies are all born within a short time. More than four can be born but this is very rare and some usually die.

Which features can you inherit from your parents?

You inherit certain special features from your parents, as well as the same general kind of body shape. Your skin colour depends on the skin colour of your parents, and so does the colour of your hair and eyes. Your face may look rather like a combination of both your parents' faces, or you may resemble one of your parents more than the other. You may inherit a disability from them, like colour blindness. You may get certain abilities, like musical ability, but this is very difficult to prove.

A family tree can help you trace inherited features in your family.

Male ■

Female ●

Your grandfather   *Your grandmother*

Your aunts   *and uncles*   *Your parents*

Your cousins   *You, your brothers and sisters*   *Cousin*

In this family, blonde hair has been passed from generation to generation.

The Senses

How many senses do you have?

You have five main senses – sight, hearing, smell, taste and touch. Balance can be thought of as another sense. You need your senses to live, though blind or deaf people are able to live well and happily without all these senses. Your senses seem to operate at the outside of your body. You feel something touching you at a certain place, or taste something on your tongue, for example. In fact, signals go from these places along nerves to your brain. You actually sense everything inside your brain.

The sensory cells that detect smells are in the nasal cavity. Those that detect taste are on the tongue.

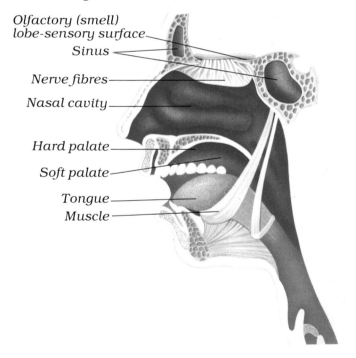

Olfactory (smell) lobe-sensory surface
Sinus
Nerve fibres
Nasal cavity
Hard palate
Soft palate
Tongue
Muscle

How can we taste?

We have about 10,000 tiny taste buds on our tongues. Certain areas of the tongue are more sensitive to some tastes than others. The four main tastes are sweet, sour, bitter and salty.

Why do your ears pop?

If you travel in an aeroplane or go up and down in a lift, you may suddenly feel your ears popping. Your hearing seems to fade, and then it suddenly comes back loud and clear with a popping sound. This happens because your ears do not like sudden changes in air pressure. These changes happen as you go up and down. When your ears pop, air moves in or out of them as they adjust to the change in air pressure.

Why do we blink?

We blink our eyes to keep them clean. You do this all the time your eyes are open without thinking about it. As your eyelids close over your eyes, they wipe a layer of water over the surface. This clears away any dust on the eyeball.

How do you keep your balance?

You know immediately if you are falling over, or even if you bend slightly to one side. If you are suddenly caught off balance, you instantly move to keep upright. Your sense of balance is located in your ears. Inside each ear are three semicircular tubes called canals. They detect when you move either up or down, backward or forward, or sideways, and send messages to your brain. Your brain 'reads' these messages to give you your sense of balance.

A gymnast balances gracefully on a bar.

Breathing

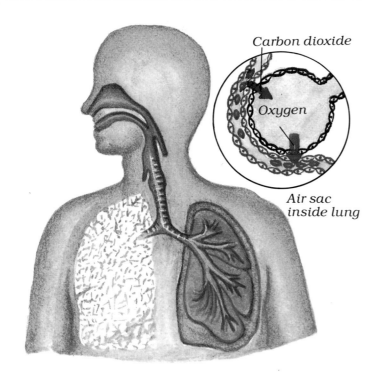

We get the oxygen we need by breathing.

What do you do with the air you breathe?

When you breathe in, your lungs expand and suck in air. When you breathe out, the lungs contract and force out air. Your lungs take oxygen from the air. The oxygen dissolves in blood channels at the surface of the lungs, and the oxygen-rich blood then goes to all parts of your body. The oxygen is used by your body to gain energy and keep you alive. This changes it into the gas carbon dioxide which is carried in your blood back to the lungs. It goes from the blood into the lungs, and is then breathed out.

How often do you breathe in and out?

If you are sitting down, you breathe in and out about twenty times every minute. That's more than 10 million times in a year. If you run or exercise your body in any other way, you breathe more quickly. You need more air to get the extra energy, and you feel out of breath and pant until you get enough air.

Why do you yawn when you get sleepy?

When you yawn, you open your mouth and gulp in quite a lot of air. This helps to refresh you, and may stop you from dropping off to sleep if you do not really need to sleep.

Why do you sometimes get hiccups?

Hiccups are usually caused by not digesting food properly. Indigestion may irritate the diaphragm, which is the large muscle that makes you breathe in and out. The diaphragm jerks, making you take a sudden sharp breath – you hiccup.

How does your voice work?

You can talk because you can make sounds with your vocal cords. These are situated in your voice box or larynx, which is in your neck at the bump called your 'Adam's apple'. The vocal cords are flaps that lie across your windpipe. They vibrate as air passes over them, and muscles continually change the vibration to produce speech. The action is rather like twanging a rubber band to give different sounds.

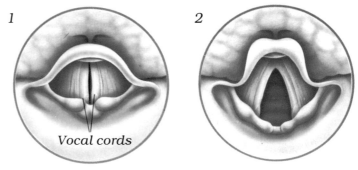

Vocal cords make high pitched sounds when they are close together (1) and low pitched sounds when they are far apart (2).

What is hay fever?

Hay fever is a condition that many people get every summer. It may occur in the spring and autumn too. Tiny pollen particles from plants float in the air. People breathe in the pollen particles, and they may cause hay fever. This produces sudden sneezing, and headaches and coughing if it is severe.

Eating and Drinking

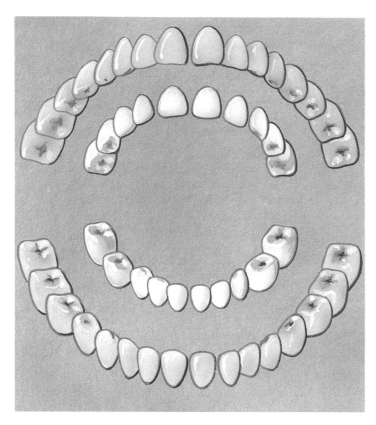

The inner rows show a child's milk teeth. The outer rows show an adult's permanent teeth.

How many teeth have you got?

This depends on how old you are. A baby has no teeth at all, but a fully-grown person has 32 permanent teeth. Before you grow these permanent teeth, you grow 20 milk teeth. The milk teeth slowly drop out, one by one, as the permanent teeth grow. All these teeth should have appeared by the time you are 25 years old.

How can sugar damage your teeth?

Eating sugar, and eating sweets that contain sugar, is not good for your teeth. Bits of sugar stay around your teeth, no matter how much you chew. Germs are always present in your mouth, and they act on the sugar to produce acid. This acid attacks the enamel covering your teeth. In time, it makes holes in the teeth.

What are false teeth made of?

If you break a tooth, the dentist can give you a false tooth to replace it. False teeth are made of materials that are strong and do not dissolve in the mouth. People once had false teeth made of ivory, rubber or gold, but nowadays dentists make them of plastics or porcelain. These materials are very tough, and they can be coloured to look exactly like real teeth.

Why is fluoride put in water?

Fluoride is a mineral that is sometimes found in water supplies. In many places, it is put into the water because many dentists believe that it is good for the teeth. Many people use toothpaste containing fluoride for the same reason. It becomes part of the enamel that covers the teeth. The fluoride makes the enamel stronger, so that the teeth will resist decay and stay healthy.

What is saliva used for?

Saliva or spit is the fluid in your mouth, and it has several uses. It helps you to swallow food by making your throat slippery. Try eating dry biscuits that soak up saliva, and see how difficult it is to swallow them. It also helps you to taste food, because substances in the food have to dissolve in the saliva for your tongue to taste them. Also, the saliva begins to digest your food.

How long does it take you to digest your food?

You begin to digest your food as soon as you eat it. It goes down your throat to your stomach. There it is covered with stomach juices, which help to change the food into substances that your body can use for body building and energy. The contents then pass into your intestines *(see next question)*, where your body absorbs the useful food substances. The whole process is called digestion. It usually takes you about four hours to digest your food. A heavy meal takes longer than a light meal or drinks.

How long are your intestines?

Your intestines are longer than you are – about $8\frac{1}{2}$ to 9 metres. They form a long tube that is coiled up inside your body. Food enters from your stomach at the top end. It passes down the intestines, and is digested. Only waste matter is left behind after digestion, and this leaves your body from the bottom end of the intestines. In all, it takes about a day for food to go completely through your body.

The digestive system

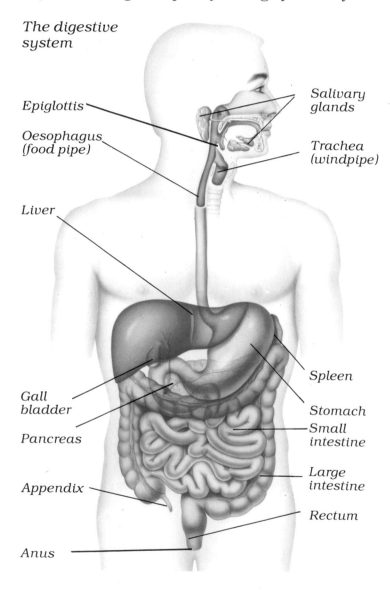

Epiglottis
Oesophagus (food pipe)
Liver
Gall bladder
Pancreas
Appendix
Anus

Salivary glands
Trachea (windpipe)
Spleen
Stomach
Small intestine
Large intestine
Rectum

Which foods contain roughage?

We need to make sure that the food we eat contains enough roughage because roughage helps to get rid of waste food. Raw vegetables and wholemeal bread are good sources of roughage.

These foods are rich in vitamins and minerals.

Why do we need vitamins and minerals?

We need minerals to help build up the body and we need vitamins to change food into energy. Foods that are rich in both vitamins and minerals are fish, milk, fruit and vegetables, bread, eggs and butter.

Which drinks contain alcohol?

Drinks like cider, beer, sherry, wine, gin and whisky contain a liquid called alcohol. Drinks such as lemonade, cola and orange juice do not contain alcohol. They are often called soft drinks, which means that they do not contain alcohol. People get drunk if they consume too much alcoholic drink.

Can you live with only one kidney?

Yes. You have two kidneys, but one will keep you alive if necessary. Your kidneys clean your blood. After your body uses food substances produced by digestion, waste substances are left in the blood. The kidneys remove them, and they go into the urine and leave the body.

Health and Medicine

How long can people live?

In countries where there is good medical care, you can expect to live on average for about 70 years if you are male, and 75 years if you are female. If you remain healthy, you may live much longer. However, only one person in about three million lives to be 100. Nobody has been known for certain to have lived beyond the age of 120.

Why do you need sleep?

If you cannot sleep, you feel tired and irritable. Once you get some sleep, you generally wake up feeling refreshed and alert. Waste substances build up in your body, and your muscles are strained during the day, making you tired. At night, while you are asleep, you are not using your body and it has a chance to grow and repair and clean itself inside.

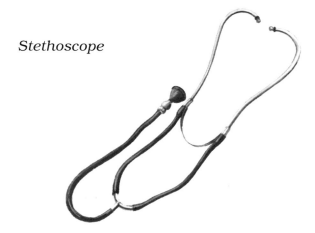

Stethoscope

What is a stethoscope used for?

A doctor may use a stethoscope to examine you. A stethoscope consists of a hollow end and two thin tubes with ear-pieces. The doctor places the end against your chest or back, and puts the ear-pieces in his or her ears. The doctor can then hear the sounds of your breathing and heartbeat, and make sure that your lungs and heart are working properly.

What is the normal temperature of your body?

The temperature inside your body is usually always the same – about 36.9°C. It is measured by putting a thermometer under your tongue. This temperature may go up or down a little with no ill effects.

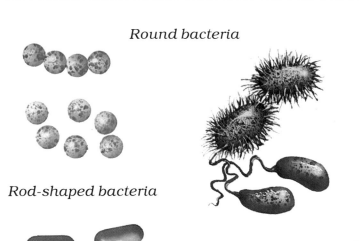

Round bacteria

Rod-shaped bacteria

These bacteria have fine threads to help them move.

What are bacteria?

Bacteria are tiny particles made up of living cells, which can move and reproduce. They can invade plants and animals and cause disease. In people, bacteria cause many diseases, including pneumonia, whooping cough, tetanus, typhoid and tuberculosis. Other bacteria may be useful to us. They are used to make cheese, and bacteria help vegetables such as beans and peas to grow.

What is acupuncture?

Acupuncture is a kind of medical treatment which can cure illness and stop pain. In acupuncture, needles are stuck into certain parts of the body. They are pushed lightly into the skin. The parts are not always the same as those parts that are affected, but may be elsewhere. The treatment often works, but no one really knows why. It comes from China.

1. A virus enters a cell.

2. New viruses are made.

3. The cell bursts open and new viruses are released.

Who discovered vaccination?

Edward Jenner, a British doctor, discovered that vaccination prevents disease in 1796. He injected a boy with fluid from a milkmaid who had cowpox. The boy got cowpox, which was not dangerous. Then Jenner injected him with smallpox, a very dangerous disease. However, the boy did not get smallpox. The cowpox fluid was a vaccine against smallpox, as Jenner had expected, and gave him resistance to smallpox. Vaccination has become the most important way of preventing disease, and it has improved people's health enormously.

What is a virus?

A virus is the smallest living thing. Viruses are particles only about a millionth of a centimetre across. In fact, a virus is not alive all the time. It comes to life only when it enters a living cell in an animal, a plant or a bacterium. Then the virus makes the cell produce more viruses. This causes disease. In people viruses cause many diseases, including colds, influenza, measles, mumps and chickenpox. Viruses are present in air, water and the soil.

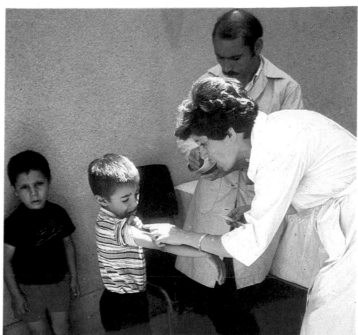

A young boy is vaccinated against tuberculosis.

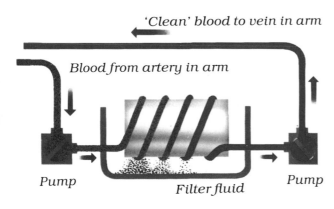

'Clean' blood to vein in arm

Blood from artery in arm

Pump

Filter fluid

Pump

This diagram shows what happens to blood when it is filtered by a kidney machine.

What is a kidney machine?

A kidney machine is a large and complex machine that can do the work of normal kidneys for people whose own kidneys have stopped working. The machine filters all the waste matter from the blood of patients connected to the machine.

Why do you have vaccinations?

Vaccinations stop you from getting certain diseases. They make you immune to those diseases. You can have vaccinations to prevent tetanus, diphtheria, measles, influenza, poliomyelitis and many other dangerous diseases. You have several vaccinations when you are young. The vaccine is either injected into you or you swallow it. It is a preparation containing viruses or bacteria that can no longer harm you. However, the body acts as if they are harmful and resists them. This resistance stays in the body, and protects you if you come into contact with the disease later.

Surgeons and nurses wear sterile clothing in the operating theatre.

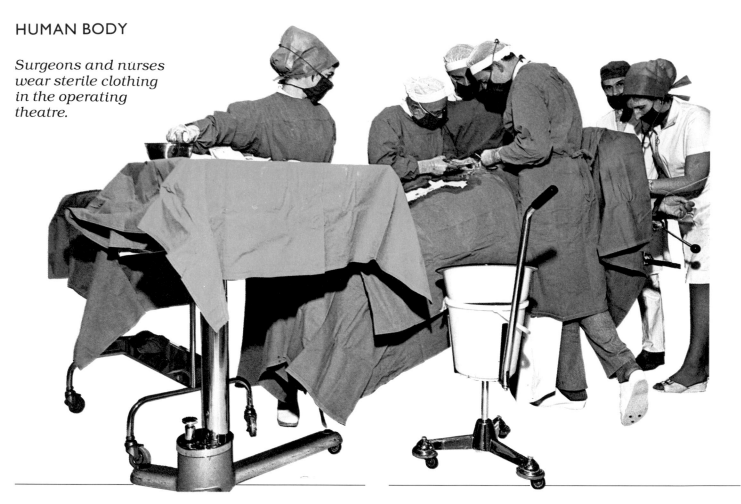

What is an epidemic?

An epidemic is an outbreak of an illness. Many people get the illness at the same time in a particular region. It lasts for a while, and then people stop falling ill. The epidemic is over, although it may occur again. An epidemic may be caused if people bring an illness to a region, and the illness then spreads quickly to the people living there. It may also be caused by a change in living conditions – for example, by a change of season or by an earthquake. However, drugs can usually prevent epidemics.

What does an anaesthetic do?

An anaesthetic is a drug that stops you feeling any pain. You have an anaesthetic if you need an operation or any treatment that is painful. A local anaesthetic stops pain in only one part of your body – for example, around a tooth that is being drilled. You have a general anaesthetic for bigger operations. It makes you unconscious during the operation. This is like being asleep, and you do not feel anything.

What is a contagious disease?

A contagious disease is a disease that you can get from another person who has the disease.

What are antibiotics?

Scientists have developed a whole range of drugs to fight disease. These are called antibiotics. They attack the germs in the body but they do not attack the body's cells.

Why do surgeons and nurses wear gowns and masks in an operating theatre?

Before doing an operation, surgeons and nurses scrub their hands with antiseptics. They then put on gowns, caps, gloves and masks to cover all the body except for the eyes. The clothes are sterile, which means that they have been treated so that they are free of bacteria. The operating theatre is cleaned to remove all bacteria too. In this way, no bacteria get into the patient during the operation where they may cause disease.

Who discovered penicillin?

Penicillin was the first antibiotic, a special drug that is very good at killing bacteria. With antibiotics, many illnesses can soon be cured that were once incurable. Penicillin was discovered by accident by the British scientist Sir Alexander Fleming in 1928. He noticed that a mould which had formed in a dish in his laboratory was killing bacteria in the dish. From the mould, penicillin was later prepared. In 1938, Howard Florey and Ernst Chain found a way to make penicillin in large quantities.

What is rabies?

Rabies is one of the most dreaded diseases. It is caught from animals – for example, by being bitten by a dog with rabies. Once the disease starts, it cannot be stopped. The patient dies in a few days in agony. Rabies no longer exists in Britain. This is because all animals that enter the country have to go into quarantine. They are kept in cages for several months to make absolutely certain that they do not have rabies.

What is frostbite?

Frostbite happens if any part of your body gets very cold. Your fingers and toes are likely to get frostbite if you spend a long time in snow and ice – if you are stranded outside in winter, for example. The cold stops the blood flowing through the flesh. If this goes on for too long, the flesh dies and may wither away. The tips of noses, fingers and toes can be lost by frostbite. However, they must get very cold for a long time for this to happen.

What is sunstroke?

Sunstroke happens because the body gets too hot. You can get sunstroke if you stay out in hot sunshine for too long. It makes your head ache and you feel tired. In bad cases, people are sick and their minds may be affected. It is cured by resting in a cool, dark room, and drinking fluids rather than eating.

Louis Pasteur

Who discovered that germs cause disease?

This great discovery was made by a French scientist, Louis Pasteur. Pasteur made several important discoveries in science, including the discovery that germs – living things so small as to be invisible – make wine and beer go sour. He thought that they might cause disease. These germs we now know to be viruses, bacteria and others. Pasteur was able to prove his ideas in 1870. They showed that cleanliness is necessary for health.

What does an antiseptic do?

An antiseptic is a substance which kills the bacteria that cause illness. Antiseptics are used to clean places where bacteria may be dangerous. Strong antiseptics called disinfectants are used to clean places where bacteria may grow – for example, toilets and drains. Mild antiseptics are used to clean cuts and grazes on the skin, and to wash the mouth and throat. All these measures stop bacteria from getting into our bodies where they can cause disease.

HISTORY

Famous Firsts

Who was the first person to travel around the world?

The first ship to sail around the world was the *Vittoria (Victoria)* commanded by the Portuguese explorer Ferdinand Magellan. The voyage took nearly three years, from 1519 to 1522. Magellan was killed during the voyage, and the 18 sailors who survived became the first people to travel around the world.

Who first climbed Mount Everest?

The summit of Mount Everest was first reached by two people – Edmund Hillary of New Zealand and Tensing Norgay of Nepal. They reached the top of the world's highest mountain on 29 May 1953.

Climbing Mount Everest

Who were the first people to leave the Earth?

The first person to fly in space was the Russian cosmonaut Yuri Gagarin in 1961. However, he did not leave the Earth's field of gravity, and simply circled the Earth once. The first spacemen to escape from the Earth's gravity and really get away from the Earth were the crew of the American spacecraft Apollo 8. In December 1968, they circled the Moon. They returned safely to Earth a few days later. The astronauts of this historic space mission were Frank Borman, James Lovell and William Anders.

Who first reached the North Pole?

There is no easy answer to this question. The American explorers Frederick Cook and Robert Peary both claimed to have reached the North Pole – the first in 1908 and the second a year later. However, it is possible that their claims are not true and that they turned back before getting to the Pole. The first person definitely to reach the North Pole was the American explorer Richard Byrd, who flew over the pole in an aircraft on 9 May 1926. The first explorer definitely to travel over the ice to the North Pole was the American explorer Ralph Plaisted. He arrived there on 19 April 1968.

Who first reached the South Pole?

The first team of explorers to reach the South Pole was led by the Norwegian explorer Roald Amundsen. Using dogs to pull their sleds, they reached the Pole on 14 December 1911.

Sir John Alcock　　　*Sir Arthur Brown*

The
*Vickers Vimy
flew non-stop
across the Atlantic.*

Who were the first people to cross Australia?

The centre of Australia is desert, and it is dangerous to try and cross it overland. The first explorers to make the journey were Robert Burke, Charles Gray and John King. With the aid of camels, they crossed Australia from south to north in 1860 and 1861.

Who first swam the English Channel?

A British sea captain, Matthew Webb, first swam across the English Channel from England to France, a distance of 34 kilometres in a straight line. His swim, in August 1875, took $21\frac{3}{4}$ hours.

Roald Amundsen reaches the South Pole.

Who first flew non-stop across the Atlantic Ocean?

Two British airmen, John Alcock and Arthur Brown, made the first non-stop flight across the Atlantic Ocean on 14–15 June 1919. It lasted nearly $16\frac{1}{2}$ hours, and Brown had to crawl out on to the wings of the aircraft to remove ice that was forming there. Tragically, Alcock was killed in an air crash only a few months later.

Who first sailed around the world alone?

An American sailor, Captain Joshua Slocum, made the first solo voyage around the world in a small sailing boat called *Spray*. The journey took three years and two months from 1895 to 1898. Slocum could not swim. He set out again in 1909, and was never seen again.

Explorers

Who discovered America, but thought he had reached India?

The first European explorer known to have reached America was Christopher Columbus, who was born in Italy, but explored for the Spanish. He sailed from Spain to the Bahama Islands off the coast of North America in 1492. However, it is likely that Viking sailors reached America long before Columbus did. Columbus was trying to find a new route to India or the Indies (then a name for the East), and thought he had got there. He therefore called the people he found there Indians, and this is how the American Indians got their name.

Who sailed across the Pacific Ocean on a raft?

In 1947, a team of scientists led by Thor Heyerdahl, who was born in Norway in 1914, sailed across the Pacific Ocean on a raft called the *Kon-Tiki.* The raft was of an ancient design, and the expedition showed that the people of the South Sea islands could have got there by raft from South America.

Who is America named after?

America is named after the Italian explorer Amerigo Vespucci, who lived from 1451 to 1512. Vespucci explored part of South America after Columbus reached America. Unlike Columbus, Vespucci believed that a new land had been discovered, and it was named America after him. The name was then given to the whole continent.

Columbus took three ships on his voyage to America, the Santa Maria, Pinta and Niña.

Who first sailed around Africa to India?

The first voyage from Europe around Africa to India was made because European traders wanted to find a sea route to India instead of going overland. It was made by the Portuguese explorer Vasco Da Gama. He left Portugal in 1497, and took nearly a year to reach India.

Who named a huge country after a tiny village?

This was the French explorer Jacques Cartier and the country is Canada. Although he was not the first European to reach Canada, Cartier was the first to explore much of it. From 1534 onwards, he made three voyages to Canada. Cartier tried to find out what the Indian name for the country was. However, the Indians he asked did not properly understand him and thought he was enquiring about their village. So they said 'kanada', which meant 'village'.

How did the river Amazon get its name?

In 1541, a Spanish explorer called Francisco de Orellana discovered a great river in South America. While tracing its course, he was attacked by a group of Indian women warriors. These reminded him of the Amazons, the women warriors in ancient Greek legends, and so he named the river the Amazon.

Why did explorers seek the Northwest Passage?

After Magellan discovered a sea route from Europe to the East around South America, explorers wondered whether there might be another route around North America. It would involve sailing through the Arctic islands north of Canada, but it would be shorter than the southern route and better for traders. Explorers sought this route – the Northwest Passage – for centuries. It was finally discovered by the Norwegian explorer Roald Amundsen in a voyage that lasted from 1903 to 1906.

Marco Polo and his travelling companions

Which part of the world did Marco Polo explore?

Marco Polo and his family were the greatest European travellers of the Middle Ages. Marco was born in Venice, Italy. His father and uncle were traders and had visited China, where they met the Emperor Kublai Khan. In 1271, they set off again with Marco. The travellers did not return until 1295. During all this time, they travelled throughout China and southern Asia.

Who first explored the South Seas?

The South Seas are the southern part of the Pacific Ocean, and are dotted with many tropical islands. This part of the world was first thoroughly explored by Captain James Cook, a British explorer who made three voyages there between 1768 and 1779. He also explored Australia and New Zealand, and he realized that a great unknown continent (Antarctica) must exist to the south, though he never reached it. Captain Cook was murdered by natives in Hawaii on his third voyage.

The conquistadors captured Montezuma, the Aztec ruler, soon after their arrival in Mexico.

Who were the conquistadors?

The conquistadors were the Spanish invaders who conquered the Indian civilizations in Central and South America in the 1500s. Conquistador is the Spanish word for 'conqueror'. The conquistadors sought the gold treasures made by the Indians but destroyed their civilizations. The best-known of the conquistadors are Hernando Cortes, who plundered Mexico, and Francisco Pizarro, who laid waste the Inca Empire of Peru.

Famous Leaders

Churchill, Roosevelt and Stalin, leaders of Great Britain, the United States and the USSR in 1945

Who led Britain in World War II?

The British leader in World War II was Winston Churchill, who lived from 1874 to 1965. Churchill became prime minister in 1940, soon after the outbreak of war. By that time, Germany had invaded most of the rest of Europe and Britain stood virtually alone against the enemy. The British forces fought strongly under Churchill's powerful leadership, and the country was not invaded. The USSR and the United States entered the war in 1941, and the war was over four years later.

Which country was led by General de Gaulle?

Charles de Gaulle was the greatest French leader of this century. He was born in 1890, and became a general early in World War II. When the Germans invaded and occupied France, de Gaulle refused to collaborate with them. He left, and commanded the Free French forces in action outside France. De Gaulle returned after the war, and was President of France from 1945 to 1946 and from 1958 to 1969.

Who was elected President of the United States four times?

Franklin D. Roosevelt was elected President of the United States four times – in 1932, 1936, 1940 and 1944. He died in 1945 having served as president for twelve years, a record. Roosevelt was a remarkable man. He led the United States through the depression of the 1930s and through World War II, yet he was crippled by polio. Now, no president is allowed to serve for more than eight consecutive years.

Who led Germany in World War II?

The German leader in World War II was Adolf Hitler. Hitler came to power in Germany in 1933 at the head of the National Socialist party. He and his followers were known as Nazis (short for National Socialists). They set up a dictatorship in Germany, killing their enemies, and began to invade other European countries. This caused World War II. Germany lost the war, and Hitler killed himself in 1945 as the war ended.

Which country was led by Kemal Ataturk?

Kemal Ataturk was the leader of Turkey from 1920 to 1938, when he died. He removed much of the influence of the Muslim religion, giving Turkey new laws based on those of European countries instead of religious laws. He also gave women freedom and even changed the alphabet, so that Turkish is now written in Roman letters, like English. These reforms made Turkey a modern nation. Ataturk's real name was Mustafa Kemal. The title Ataturk means 'father of the Turks'.

Which political movement follows the teachings of Karl Marx?

Karl Marx was born in Germany in 1818 and died in Britain in 1883. He was not a ruler, but his ideas have had a tremendous influence on the world in this century. Marx wrote *The Communist Manifesto* and *Das Kapital (Capital)*. These works founded the communist movement, which came to power in Russia in 1917.

Prince Otto von Bismarck   *Sitting Bull*

Who was known as 'the little corporal'?

Napoleon Bonaparte (1769–1821) was a Corsican soldier who crowned himself emperor of France in 1804. He was eventually defeated by British and Prussian forces at the Battle of Waterloo in 1815 and was exiled to the island of St Helena. Napoleon was not very tall and was known affectionately as 'the little corporal' by his soldiers.

Who was Sitting Bull?

Sitting Bull was a fierce leader of the Sioux Indians in the United States. He lived from about 1834 to 1890. So that they would not lose all their lands, Sitting Bull persuaded the Sioux to fight and kill the white settlers. This led to the famous Battle of Little Bighorn in 1876, when the Indians slaughtered Colonel George Custer and his troops. This was the Indians' greatest victory. Sitting Bull survived the battle, but was driven into Canada. He later returned to the United States and, still rebellious, was killed while resisting arrest.

Who was known as the Iron Chancellor?

Prince Otto von Bismarck, who created the nation of Germany, was known as the Iron Chancellor. Bismarck was born in 1815, when Germany was not one country but a league of separate states. He became chief minister of Prussia, the most powerful state. Then in a series of wars, he united the states in 1871 into one Germany, of which he became Chancellor (prime minister). Because Bismarck said that problems should be settled by 'blood and iron', he became known as the Iron Chancellor. He led Germany until 1890.

The Battle of Waterloo

The Ancient World

*The empire of
Alexander the Great*

Who founded the ancient city of Alexandria?

The city of Alexandria in Egypt was founded in 331 BC by the Greek Emperor Alexander the Great. By conquest, Alexander built up a great empire that extended from Greece as far as India and Egypt, and was as big as the United States. The Empire brought Greek civilization to the ancient world, and Alexandria became its centre of learning.

Which Greek philosopher was condemned to die by drinking poison?

The Greek philosopher Socrates met this unusual death at about the age of 70 in 399 BC. Socrates was a great philosopher who liked to try to find the truth by questioning the opinions of people, often showing them to be wrong. He always tried to use reason, but his method made him many enemies. Eventually, he was condemned to death. When his jailer brought him the cup of poison, he drank it calmly.

Who was the first Roman emperor?

Augustus, who lived from 63 BC to AD 14, was the first emperor of ancient Rome. Before Augustus, Rome was a republic governed by consuls, who were elected to power. After the death of Julius Caesar, Augustus – then called Octavian – held power with Mark Antony. Octavian defeated Mark Antony, and in 27 BC declared that Rome would henceforth be an empire with himself as the first emperor. He took the name Augustus, and Rome reached its greatest glory under his rule. The month of August is named after him.

*Augustus, the
first Roman emperor*

Which queen fascinated both Julius Caesar and Mark Antony?

Cleopatra was an extremely beautiful queen of Egypt. She was born in 69 BC. The Roman leader Julius Caesar, fascinated by her, used his power to make her queen. After Caesar's death, Cleopatra captivated Mark Antony, his successor. Antony left his wife Octavia for Cleopatra, provoking a battle for control of Rome with Octavian, who was Octavia's brother and leader of Rome with Mark Antony. Octavian met Antony and Cleopatra in battle in 31 BC and won. Antony killed himself and Cleopatra tried to charm Octavian. Failing to do so, she too killed herself – possibly with an asp (a poisonous snake).

Why did the Emperor Hadrian build a wall right across England?

Hadrian's Wall is a famous landmark in the north of England. It is a huge wall, 118 kilometres long, that runs across the whole country from coast to coast. It was built by the Roman Emperor Hadrian between AD 123 and 138 to keep Scottish raiders from invading England, then a province of the Roman Empire.

Who took a force of elephants across the Alps?

Hannibal commanded the forces of Carthage against Rome, and used elephants in war to scare his enemies. Hannibal took the Romans by surprise by marching over the Alps in 218 BC, taking the elephants with him. Once in Italy, Hannibal harried the Romans for years but he did not defeat them.

What is Stonehenge?

Stonehenge is an ancient monument in southern England, and it was built at various times between 2750 BC and 1500 BC. It was probably used as a temple, or to observe the movements of the Sun and Moon to make calendars.

Why did the ancient Egyptians build the pyramids?

The pyramids were built as tombs for the pharaohs (rulers) of ancient Egypt, and they had chambers that contained the remains of the pharaohs. However, these chambers were later robbed of their treasures. The biggest pyramid, the Great Pyramid, was 146.5 metres high when it was built in about 2600 BC, but it is now slightly smaller.

What was the Holy Roman Empire?

The Holy Roman Empire was a group of small German and neighbouring states that were powerful in the Middle Ages. It was intended to be a second Roman Empire built of Christian states. The Empire was founded by Charlemagne or Charles the Great, who was crowned the first Holy Roman Emperor by the Pope in Rome on Christmas Day, AD 800. The Empire lasted until 1806, when the French Emperor Napoleon conquered most of Germany.

What were the seven wonders of the world?

The seven wonders were structures of the ancient world. They were considered to be the seven most wonderful ever built. The Great Pyramid in Egypt is the only one still standing. The other six were the Hanging Gardens of Babylon (Iraq); the Temple of Diana at Ephesus (Turkey); the Tomb of Mausolus at Halicarnassus (Turkey); the statue of Jupiter at Olympia (Greece); the Pharos Lighthouse at Alexandria (Egypt); and the Colossus of Rhodes (Greece), a statue so big that it may have straddled the harbour entrance so that ships passed beneath its legs.

Thousands of workers hauled huge stone blocks to build the pyramids.

119

Famous Events

Which event is commemorated by the Eiffel Tower in Paris?

The Eiffel Tower, designed by Alexandre Eiffel, was built for the Paris Exhibition of 1889. This exhibition commemorated the French Revolution, which began a century before. The Revolution started on 14 July 1789, when a mob of angry people attacked the Bastille, a prison in Paris. They actually pulled the building down stone by stone and set the prisoners free. The anniversary of the destruction of the Bastille is now a national holiday throughout France.

Who fought at the Battle of Verdun in 1916?

Verdun was the site of a major battle in World War I. In a six month struggle, French forces held an attack by German armies commanded by Crown Prince William. French losses were 348,000 men, and German losses 328,000 men.

Eiffel Tower

The sinking of the Titanic *is one of the greatest disasters in maritime history.*

Which great ship, said to be unsinkable, sank on its maiden voyage?

This ship was the *Titanic*, a British passenger liner. At the time, the *Titanic* was the world's largest ship, and experts believed that it was unsinkable. But on the night of 14 April 1912, during its first voyage, it hit an iceberg in the middle of the Atlantic Ocean. It sank and, out of more than 2200 people on board, over 1500 were drowned.

Who was shot at Ford's Theatre, Washington, in 1865?

Abraham Lincoln, sixteenth President of the United States, was shot on 14 April 1865 at Ford's Theatre, Washington. He died the next day. He was shot by an unsuccessful actor called John Wilkes Booth, who wanted to kill Lincoln because the Confederate States had been beaten in the American Civil War.

When was President Kennedy of the United States assassinated?

President John F. Kennedy was assassinated by a gunman in Dallas, Texas on 22 November 1963 while driving in an open car.

The Confederate soldiers withdrew after the Battle of Williamsburg in 1862.

Which war became known as the Great War?

World War I (1914–1918) became known as the Great War. This was because, at the time, there had never been another war in which so many different countries took part. More people were killed than ever before in a war, and more buildings were destroyed. But, when World War II took place (1939–1945), it was even bigger.

What was the Hundred Years' War?

France and England were at war from 1337 to 1453. This is more than a hundred years but the period is known as the Hundred Years' War. It was eventually won by France.

What happened at Dien Bien Phu in 1954?

French influence came to an end in Indochina when the French surrendered to Vietminh troops after a siege which lasted eight weeks. The event also marked the beginning of the long struggle between North and South Vietnam which led to the Vietnam War.

Which war was fought by the Union (or the North) and the Confederacy (or the South)?

This war was the American Civil War. In 1861, eleven Southern States left the American Union rather than accept a president (Abraham Lincoln) who was supported by the Northern States. The main disagreement between the Union and the Confederacy (the Southern States) was the problem of slavery. The South supported slavery and the North was against it. The American Civil War started in April 1861. The fighting continued until 1865 and the North was victorious. Slavery was abolished and the Southern States rejoined the Union.

How long did the Vietnam War last?

The Vietnam War began in 1957 between North Vietnam and South Vietnam. America joined the war on the side of South Vietnam and the fighting did not end until 1975, when South Vietnam surrendered to North Vietnam. The war therefore lasted for 18 years. North and South Vietnam reunified in 1976.

What does the Bayeux Tapestry show?

The Bayeux Tapestry is a very long piece of embroidery. It shows in pictures the invasion of England by Duke William of Normandy (William the Conqueror) in 1066. Bayeux is a small town in northern France and the Tapestry is in a museum there. It is rather like a strip cartoon, and it starts with King Harold of England's visit to Duke William, probably in 1064. It ends with the Battle of Hastings in 1066 when Harold was killed by an arrow which pierced his eye.

A section of the Bayeux Tapestry showing the defeat of King Harold

Boston Tea Party

What was the Charge of the Light Brigade?

Between 1854 and 1856 the Crimean War was fought between Russia on one side and Turkey, England, France and Sardinia on the other. In October 1854, the Russians tried to seize the British base at Balaklava. Owing to a misunderstanding of orders the Light Brigade, an army division, charged the main Russian position. The soldiers were heavily outnumbered by the Russians and many were killed, but they got through and captured the position.

Which war began with a tea party?

In 1773, when America was still a British colony, a Tea Act was passed in Britain which allowed the East India Company to send tea directly from London to America without using American merchants. In Boston, a group of patriotic Americans disguised themselves as Indians, boarded the tea ships, and threw the tea into the harbour. This event is known as the Boston Tea Party and marked the beginning of the American War of Independence.

Why do Americans celebrate the Fourth of July?

In 1776, the fourth of July was the day on which the 13 North American colonies declared themselves free and independent of Britain. The American Revolution, or War of Independence, broke out in 1775. The colonists were very dissatisfied with the British government and fighting started at Lexington in April 1775. The Declaration of Independence was adopted in 1776 but the war continued until 1781, when the British surrendered at Yorktown. In America, the fourth of July is called Independence Day and is a national holiday.

Signing the Declaration of Independence

Why is the year 1901 important in the history of Australia?

On 1 January 1901, the Commonwealth of Australia came into being. Before this, Australia consisted of a number of separate colonies. By the Commonwealth Act of 1900, the colonies became a federation. The formation of the Commonwealth marked the beginning of Australia as a full nation.

What happened at Gettysburg in 1863?

The Federal forces under George Meade defeated Robert E. Lee's Confederate army, marking a turning point in the American Civil War.

Famous Rulers

Who was Good Queen Bess?

Queen Elizabeth I of England is sometimes called Good Queen Bess. She was the daughter of King Henry VIII and Anne Boleyn, and became queen when her half-sister Mary I died in 1558. During Elizabeth's reign England became a great nation. She died in 1603.

Who was known as the Sun King?

Louis XIV of France was known as the Sun King. He became king in 1643 when he was only five years old. He was called the Sun King because his court was so splendid. He had a magnificent palace and gardens built at Versailles near Paris. He remained king for 72 years and died in 1715.

Louis XIV looks at plans for the palace at Versailles.

Who built the Taj Mahal?

One of the most beautiful buildings in the world, the Taj Mahal, was built at Agra in northern India by the Emperor Shah Jehan. It took 20,000 workmen about 18 years to complete (1630–1648), and was a tomb for his wife.

Which king of England had six wives?

This famous king was Henry VIII. In 1509, he married Catherine of Aragon. He divorced her in 1533 and married Anne Boleyn. In 1536, he had Anne beheaded and immediately married Jane Seymour. Unfortunately she died the following year. His fourth wife was Anne of Cleves. He married her in 1540, disliked her, and divorced her six months later. In the same year he married Catherine Howard, only to have her beheaded less than two years later. His sixth wife, Catherine Parr, luckily managed to outlive him!

Which queen was known as 'the grandmother of Europe'?

Queen Victoria became queen of Great Britain and Ireland in 1837. She reigned for nearly 64 years until her death in 1901, at the age of 81. In 1840, Victoria married Prince Albert of Saxe-Coburg. Because of her own marriage and those of her children, she was related to most of the Royal Families of Europe and became known as 'the grandmother of Europe'.

Which country was ruled by tsars?

Tsar, or czar, was the title of Russian emperors from Ivan IV in 1547 until Nicholas II in 1918. The word probably comes from the Latin word *caesar*, meaning emperor. Nicholas II, the last tsar, was forced to abdicate during the Revolution of 1917.

Who was Ivan the Terrible?

Ivan IV, first tsar of Russia, was known as Ivan the Terrible because he became a fierce and cruel tyrant. He reigned from 1547 to 1584.

Which emperor ceased to be a god in 1946?

Before 1946, there was a tradition in Japan that the emperor was divine, that is, that he was like a god. After Japan surrendered at the end of World War II in 1945, Emperor Hirohito was allowed to remain. There were many changes in Japan in order to make it more modern and more like western countries. On 1 January 1946, Emperor Hirohito announced that the emperor no longer claimed to be divine.

Which empire was ruled by Genghis Khan?

In 1206 a chieftain called Temujin became emperor of the Mongol peoples. He took the name Genghis or Jenghiz Khan. The Mongol Empire covered much of Asia, and before he died, Genghis Khan had conquered all the lands between the Yellow River and the Red Sea.

Genghis Khan

Nicholas II, last tsar of Russia, with his family

Whose horse was called Bucephalus?

Alexander the Great became king of Macedonia in 336 BC when he was only twenty. As a boy of fourteen, he tamed a wild horse, Bucephalus, which no one else could master. He rode Bucephalus in all his battles, and when the horse died of wounds in India, Alexander built a town and named it after him.

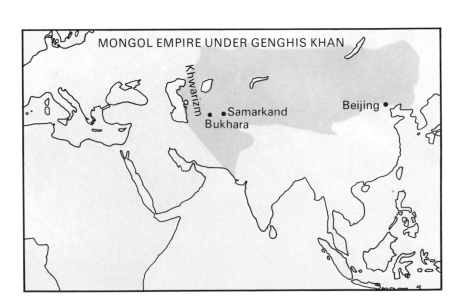

MONGOL EMPIRE UNDER GENGHIS KHAN

Khwarizm

Samarkand
Bukhara

Beijing

Napoleon places the crown on his head.

Who crowned himself emperor of France?

On 2 December 1804, Napoleon Bonaparte was to be crowned emperor of France. Pope Pius VII came to the magnificent ceremony at Notre Dame Cathedral in Paris. After the Pope had blessed him, Napoleon took the crown from him and placed it on his own head. He then crowned his wife, Josephine. Napoleon did this in order to show that he was independent of the Church.

Which king tried to make the waves obey him?

King Canute of Denmark and Norway became king of England in 1016. It is said that he tried to make the waves obey him by commanding the tide to turn back as it was coming in. Of course, he failed.

Which emperor was called the Lion of Judah?

The emperor of Ethiopia had many titles and among them he was called 'Conquering Lion of the tribe of Judah'. This was usually shortened to 'Lion of Judah'. In the Bible, Judah was the kingdom in Israel ruled by the House of David. The last Emperor of Ethiopia was Haile Selassie. He lost the throne in 1974. Ethiopia was ruled by the army until rebels formed a new government in 1991.

Which great ruler once worked as a shipbuilder?

Peter the Great of Russia visited Germany, Holland, Austria and England in the late 1600s. He had a passion for ships and worked in shipyards in Holland and England.

Where was the Ottoman Empire?

At its height, the Ottoman Empire extended from eastern Europe to North Africa. It was ruled by Turkey and was founded by Sultan Osman or Othman I, who reigned from 1288 to 1320. The Ottoman Empire lasted until the Sultans were abolished in 1922. In 1923, Turkey became a republic with Kemal Ataturk as its president.

King Canute commanding the waves

Government

What is the United Nations?

The United Nations Organization, usually called the UN, is a group of many countries that joined together in 1945 to try to encourage peace in the world. The UN has 166 member countries, and its headquarters are in New York. The UN sometimes sends special forces to try and settle quarrels between countries. There are also several UN agencies, or international organizations, that deal with international social and economic problems.

What is the Commonwealth?

When people talk about the Commonwealth, they usually mean the British Commonwealth of Nations. This is an association of nations which were once part of the British Empire. The British monarch is head of the Commonwealth, but the member countries are independent and govern themselves.

What is a republic?

A republic is a country in which the electorate (people allowed to vote) have the power to govern the country. The country is ruled by elected leaders. In some countries there is one central government, as in France. In others, there are several separate states, as in the United States and Australia. These are called *federal* republics. The head of a republic is often called the president.

How many states are there in the United States?

The United States of America is a federal republic consisting of fifty states. Most of the states are next to each other in North America but Alaska is separated from the rest by Canada, and Hawaii is an island group in the Pacific Ocean. The American flag has fifty stars on it. Each star represents one state.

What does an ambassador do?

An ambassador is a person chosen by a country to represent it in another country. The ambassador lives in an embassy. He talks to the rulers and other important people in the country on behalf of the government of his own country.

What is a dictator?

A dictator is a ruler of a country who has total power over its people. In a country ruled by a dictator, a dictatorship, there is usually only one official political party and no opposition is allowed. A dictatorship is often ruled by the army.

What is the European Community?

The European Community, often called the Common Market or the EC, is an organization of several European countries. The aim of the community is to remove customs barriers between the member countries to encourage trading, and to try to develop a common policy on farming and transport. From 1992 the Community did away with all trade barriers between members. At present it has 12 members, with other countries waiting to join.

A meeting of the European Parliament in Strasbourg, France

Religion

Which Christian religion has the most followers?

The Roman Catholic Church has more followers than any other Christian religion in the world. Roman Catholics believe that the Pope is the successor of St Peter, the apostle appointed by Jesus Christ to be head of His church. The centre of the Roman Catholic Church is Vatican City, in Rome in Italy.

Which religions teach that people return to Earth after death?

Some religions teach that, after death, the soul or spirit of a human being enters another body, human or animal. This belief is called reincarnation. Buddhists and Hindus, who live mainly in India, believe that their behaviour in this life decides in what form they will be reborn. Some people believe that a person may be reborn many times until the soul is ready to enter heaven.

Which religion follows the teachings of the Koran?

The Koran is the holy book of Islam. In Islam, there is one god called Allah, and the Koran is believed to be the word of Allah which was revealed to Muhammad by the Angel Gabriel. The religion is sometimes called Muhammadanism, and its followers are known as Muslims.

Symbols of world religions: (1) Hindu god (2) Jewish menorah (3) Christian cross (4) Shinto temple (5) Islamic crescent moon (6) Buddha

A statue of Buddha in a temple, Bangkok

Who was Buddha?

Buddha, or 'the enlightened one', is the title given to Siddhartha Gautama, an Indian holy man who lived in the 500s BC. Buddha is believed to have sat under a tree called the Bo-Tree, and come to understand the cause and cure of suffering. The followers of Buddha are called Buddhists. They live mainly in South-East Asia, China and Japan.

Who is the head of the Church of England?

The king or queen of Great Britain is head of the Church of England. When Henry VIII quarrelled with the Pope about wanting a divorce, he declared that the sovereign was head of the English church, and this was later established by law.

What is a rabbi?

A rabbi is a specially ordained official who decides upon questions of law and ceremony in the Jewish religion, or Judaism. The rabbi performs marriages and other ceremonies and is similar to a priest in Christian religions.

1 *2* *3* *4*  *5* *6*

THE ARTS

Painting and Sculpture

What is the difference between a mural and a fresco?

A mural is a picture that is painted on a wall of a building. Murals may also be painted on ceilings. A fresco is a special kind of wall painting that is made when the wall is plastered. Paints are mixed with the wet plaster as it is applied to the wall. The colours show up brightly when the plaster dries.

What is an engraving?

Engraving is a way of making a print from a picture. The picture is made by cutting lines in the surface of a plate or block. The plate or block is usually metal, though other materials such as wood can be used. The plate or block is then inked and pressed on to some paper, and a print of the picture is made.

How do sculptors make statues?

Sculptors make stone statues by carving them from a block of stone with a chisel. Many statues are made of metal, particularly bronze, which is weather resistant. These statues are first made in clay and not metal. The sculptor makes a clay statue by hand, and then produces a mould of it by placing a material such as plaster around it. The plaster sets and the original statue is removed, leaving a mould – a hole that is the exact shape of the statue. Molten bronze is then poured into the mould, and it solidifies to form a bronze statue.

Who painted the *Mona Lisa*?

Mona Lisa is the name of a famous painting by the Italian artist Leonardo da Vinci. It was painted in about 1500.

A statue of St George by the sculptor Donatello

Who were the Impressionists?

The Impressionists were a group of French painters who lived at the end of the 1800s. Instead of painting a scene exactly as it appeared, these artists painted their own impression of it. The paintings have rough outlines and brush strokes, and are often light in colour. In this way, the artists tried to catch the quality of light in a scene. Leading Impressionist painters included Claude Monet, Edouard Manet, Camille Pissarro, Edgar Degas and Pierre Renoir.

Which artist took four years to finish his most famous painting?

One of the greatest artists the world has seen was Michelangelo, who lived in Italy from 1475 to 1564. He was both a painter and sculptor. His greatest painting covers the ceiling of the Sistine Chapel in the Vatican, Rome. It consists of scenes from the Bible, and Michelangelo painted it all by himself, lying flat on scaffolding. It took him four years, from 1508 to 1512.

Why did Turner have himself tied to the mast of a ship during a storm?

The British painter Joseph Turner, who lived from 1775 to 1851, is renowned for his landscape paintings. His paintings have marvellous effects of colour that capture the play of light on a scene, for example a sunset or a storm. In order to see what a storm at sea really looks like, Turner once had himself tied to the mast of a ship that was sailing through a storm.

Who painted himself for forty years?

Many artists like to paint themselves. The most revealing of all self-portraits are those by the Dutch artist Rembrandt van Rijn, who lived from 1606 to 1669. Rembrandt was a superb painter. His paintings have a beautiful quality of light, and his portraits capture people's expressions to suggest their inner feelings. Among the best of Rembrandt's portraits are those of himself, which he painted over a period of forty years.

Who were 'the wild beasts'?

Les Fauves, or 'the wild beasts', was a name given to a group of French painters in 1905. They included Henri Matisse, André Derain, Maurice Vlaminck, Georges Rouault and Albert Marquet. Their paintings were so violent in colour and had such distorted forms that a critic called them wild beasts, and the name stuck.

Whose most famous painting is *Sunflowers*?

The Dutch painter Vincent Van Gogh is famous for his vivid paintings of landscapes, people and still-life. They are painted in broad strokes of strong colour. *Sunflowers* has become one of his most popular and famous works.

Which great Spanish artist lived most of his life in France?

Pablo Picasso was born in Spain in 1881, and lived most of his life in France, where he died in 1973. Picasso explored many styles of painting. He is regarded by many people as the greatest artist of this century.

Pablo Picasso

Music

Part of the score from Bach's Brandenburg Concertos

What is a musical score?

A score is the music that the conductor of an orchestra reads. It has all the parts that the musicians play, and the conductor has to read them all at once as he conducts. When a composer writes music, he first writes a score with all the parts in it. Then the parts for each musician are copied from it. The score may have parts for singers too.

What does being in tune mean?

Music does not sound very good if it is played out of tune. All good musicians and singers play and sing in tune. If you are out of tune, you do not produce exactly the right notes. If the notes are a little too high in pitch, they are said to be sharp. If they are a little too low, they are flat. To make sure they are in tune, orchestras tune up before they start to play.

How many notes are there in an octave?

Notes that are an octave apart on an instrument have the same letter naming them. The distance between one C and the next is an octave. If you play a scale from one to the other, the octave is the eighth note of the scale. This is why it is called an octave; it comes from the Greek word *okto* meaning 'eight'.

What are brass instruments?

Instruments are members of the brass family because of the way they are played, and not because they are made of brass. You get a sound by pressing your lips together into a mouthpiece and blowing through them. In fact, the instruments are made of metal and often of brass. Brass instruments include the trumpet, cornet, horn, trombone, euphonium and tuba.

Are woodwind instruments made of wood?

The instruments of the woodwind family include the recorder, piccolo, flute, clarinet, oboe, bassoon and saxophone. Most of them are wooden instruments, but saxophones are always made of metal and there are many metal flutes. Recorders are often made of plastic. All these instruments are in the same family because they produce a sound in the same way, and they have holes down the side to give different notes.

Brass instruments
French horn
Trombone
Cello
String instruments
Trumpet
Double bass
Violin
Woodwind instruments
Clarinet
Flute
Kettle drum
Cymbals
Percussion instruments
Drums

What is the difference between a piano, a harpsichord and an organ?

All these instruments have the same kind of keyboard, but have different sounds. This is because different things happen when you press a key. In a piano, a soft hammer strikes a taut wire and in a harpsichord, a quill plucks the wire. In an organ, a stream of air is sent through an organ pipe to make a sound. In an electronic organ, the key is a kind of switch that switches on a sound.

Does a soprano sing higher or lower than a contralto?

A soprano can sing higher than a contralto, and a contralto lower than a soprano. Soprano and contralto are usually women's voices, but boys can sing in these ranges too.

What is chamber music?

Chamber music is a kind of classical music that is played by either one instrument, or a small group of instruments. A singer or small group of singers also perform chamber music. It is called chamber music because it is music that can be performed in a chamber or room in a house. In fact, much chamber music is performed in concert halls.

How many strings does a guitar have?

The Spanish guitar and the usual kind of electric guitar both have six strings. The bass guitar has four strings, and there is also a twelve-string guitar. The twelve strings are usually tuned in six pairs.

How can bagpipes play without stopping?

Bagpipes are a set of pipes with a bag containing the air to blow them. The bag is filled with air either by blowing into it through another pipe, or by operating a small bellows beneath one arm. The bag is then squeezed gently to produce a continuous stream of air and make the pipes sound without pausing.

How many composers are called Bach?

Four famous German composers of the same family are called Bach, but the greatest and one of the finest composers the world has seen was Johann Sebastian Bach. He lived from 1685 to 1750. Bach composed music of all kinds, and did so with amazing skill and originality. His genius as a composer was not widely recognized until long after his death. While he lived, he had a great reputation as an organist.

Chamber music as it was performed in the 1700s

Ludwig van Beethoven

Which composer wrote some of the greatest music even though he was deaf?

The German composer Ludwig van Beethoven, who lived from 1770 to 1827, began to go deaf when he was about 30 years old. Although he had to stop playing, Beethoven could still compose music because he could hear it in his head and write it down exactly. This music is judged by many people to be among the finest music ever composed.

Who wrote the *Fireworks Music* and the *Water Music*?

These two famous pieces of music were composed by George Frederick Handel, who was born in Germany in 1685 but lived most of his life in Britain, where he died in 1759. The *Water Music* was written to accompany a royal procession on the river Thames in London, and the *Fireworks Music* was composed for a special fireworks display in London.

Who composed the *Unfinished Symphony*?

The *Unfinished Symphony* is the title given to the eighth symphony composed by Franz Schubert, an Austrian composer (1797–1828). It is called the *Unfinished Symphony* because Schubert wrote only two movements (sections) of this symphony, instead of the usual four movements.

Which composer caused a sensation with a ballet called *The Rite of Spring*?

The Rite of Spring is a ballet with music by the Russian composer Igor Stravinsky, who was born in Russia in 1882 and died in the United States in 1971. There was a riot at its first performance in 1913, because people disliked Stravinsky's savage music and the strange dancing of the ballet. Stravinsky had to escape from the theatre through a window. However, the music was soon recognized as a masterpiece, and it is now often performed on its own.

Who wrote an opera about a magic flute?

The Magic Flute is an opera by Wolfgang Amadeus Mozart, an Austrian composer who lived from 1756 to 1791. The story of the opera is about a magic flute that protects its owner, a prince, from evil. Mozart composed other operas and also many symphonies and other pieces of music. He wrote his first pieces when he was only six years old.

Mozart gave peformances when he was very young.

A scene from
The Ring

Richard Wagner

Who composed an opera lasting four days?

The Nibelung's Ring, or *The Ring* for short, is a set of four operas by the German composer Richard Wagner, who lived from 1813 to 1883. The four operas together make up one story about a magic ring based on old German legends. To perform the whole of *The Ring* takes four days, one opera being performed each evening.

Which famous musical is based on *Romeo and Juliet*?

The musical *West Side Story* is based on *Romeo and Juliet* by Shakespeare. Instead of taking place in Italy in the 1500s, as in Shakespeare's play, the story takes place in New York in the 1950s. The music was composed by the American composer Leonard Bernstein in 1958.

Who were the Beatles?

This group was the most successful of all groups in popular music. They achieved world-wide fame during the 1960s. The four members, all British, were John Lennon, Paul McCartney, George Harrison and Ringo Starr. John Lennon was shot dead in New York in December 1980.

Who was known as 'Satchmo'?

'Satchmo' was the nickname of the famous American jazz trumpeter Louis Armstrong, who lived from 1900 to 1971. It is short for Satchelmouth. Armstrong was the first jazz musician to become world famous. People loved his marvellous trumpet solos and the gruff sound of his singing.

Who composed *Rhapsody in Blue*?

The American pianist and popular composer George Gershwin wrote this music when he was 25. His other compositions include the opera *Porgy and Bess.*

The Beatles: Paul McCartney, George Harrison, Ringo Starr and John Lennon

Literature

What happened to the ugly duckling?

The Ugly Duckling is the title of a famous story by the great Danish story-teller Hans Christian Andersen. It is about a duckling that looks so ugly that the other ducklings mock it. However, the ugly duckling is not really a duckling at all, but a baby swan. While all the other ducklings grow up and become ducks, the ugly duckling turns into a beautiful swan.

Who were Daedalus and Icarus?

According to a Greek legend, Daedalus and his son Icarus were imprisoned by King Minos of Crete. They tried to escape by making wings of wax and feathers which they fastened on to their shoulders. The story goes that they flew over the sea like birds. Icarus, however, soared so near to the Sun that the wax on his wings melted and he plunged to his death.

Who wrote *The Three Musketeers*?

The famous novel about the adventures of three comrades was written by Alexandre Dumas the French novelist. Another of his works is *The Count of Monte Cristo*, a classic adventure story. Dumas died in 1870.

Which book by Lewis Carroll is based on a game of chess?

Through the Looking Glass, by Lewis Carroll, is based on a game of chess. It follows on from his famous book *Alice's Adventures in Wonderland*. In *Through the Looking Glass*, Alice finds a strange land on the other side of a looking glass. Chess pieces are real people there, and Alice becomes involved in a chess game with them.

A scene from Alice's Adventures in Wonderland – *Alice in the garden with the King and Queen of Hearts*

Who wanted everything he touched to turn to gold?

There is a Greek legend about a miserly king called Midas who liked gold so much that he wanted everything he touched to be turned into gold. His wish was granted by a messenger from the gods, and everything – tables, chairs, flowers – changed into solid gold. Midas was delighted until he found out that the food he touched turned into gold too so he went hungry.

Who won the race between the hare and the tortoise?

The story of the hare and the tortoise is one of Aesop's Fables, a collection of tales supposed to have been written by a Greek slave called Aesop who lived in about 600 BC. The fables are about animals, but they are really meant to show people how silly they can be. In the story of the hare and the tortoise, the two animals have a race. The tortoise wins, even though it is slower, because the hare thinks it will win easily and does not bother to run until it is too late. The meaning of the story is that slow and steady work gets results.

Who is the greatest English writer?

William Shakespeare, who lived from 1564 to 1616, was a poet and playwright. He is generally considered to be the greatest writer in English literature. The works of Shakespeare are famous in many languages and are a major influence in literature throughout the world.

Which great story-teller really wanted to be a famous actor?

The Danish author Hans Christian Andersen, who lived from 1805 to 1875, is famous for his fairy tales and stories. However, when he was young, he really wanted to become a famous actor. He went to Copenhagen to fulfil his ambition, but was rejected. He turned to writing, and wrote some of the best-loved children's stories. They include *The Emperor's New Clothes*, *The Red Shoes*, *The Tinderbox*, *The Snow Queen*, *The Princess and the Pea* and *The Ugly Duckling*.

Who wrote the great Russian novel *War and Peace*?

Count Leo Nikolayevich Tolstoy took over four years to write this magnificent novel. He wrote throughout his long life and his works include the tragic novel *Anna Karenina*. Leo Tolstoy died in 1910 when he was 82.

Which famous writer died in the South Seas?

The Scottish writer Robert Louis Stevenson settled in Samoa in the South Seas because of poor health and died there in 1894. His most popular works include *Treasure Island* and *Kidnapped*, both adventure novels.

Which children's story tells of a wooden puppet that comes to life?

Pinocchio. The author of this world famous story was Carlo Lorenzini, an Italian writer who wrote under the name Carlo Collodi.

William Shakespeare

Many of Shakespeare's plays were first performed in the Globe Theatre, London.

Who wrote *The Iliad* and *The Odyssey*?

The Iliad and *The Odyssey* are two great poems that were written in ancient Greece about 3000 years ago. They are both thought to be the work of the poet Homer. *The Iliad* tells exciting stories of the Trojan Wars, and particularly of the soldier Achilles, who could only be killed by a wound in his heel. *The Odyssey* tells of the amazing adventures of the hero Odysseus or Ulysses on his return home after the Wars.

Don Quixote rides out to battle with imaginary villains.

Is Dante's *Divine Comedy* really funny?

No. The *Divine Comedy* is a vision of heaven and hell by the Italian poet Dante Alighieri, who lived from 1265 to 1321. Dante expresses his thoughts on humanity in this way, and his great poem is very serious. Although the word comedy now means a story or play that is funny or light-hearted, it originally meant a work that is not tragic. Dante called his poem a comedy because it ends happily in heaven.

Who was Tom Thumb?

Tom Thumb was a famous dwarf, both real and imaginary. He was the hero of a story called *The History of Tom Thumbe* published in England in 1621, and real midgets were later called Tom Thumb after this story.

Who was helped by the seven dwarfs?

The seven dwarfs tried to hide Snow White, a lovely princess, from her stepmother, the queen, who was jealous of Snow White's beauty and wished to kill her. The story of *Snow White and the Seven Dwarfs* is one of many folk tales collected by two German brothers, Jacob and Wilhelm Grimm. They published their first collection of these fairy tales in 1812.

Who wrote the novel *Don Quixote*?

This classic novel was written by Saavedra Miguel de Cervantes, the Spanish writer (1547–1617). *Don Quixote* was Cervantes' greatest creation. It concerns the adventures of an eccentric knight and his servant Sancho Panza.

Who travelled around the world in eighty days?

Around the World in Eighty Days is the title of an exciting adventure story by the French writer Jules Verne. It was published in 1873. The hero of the story is Phineas Fogg, who undertakes a bet that he cannot travel right around the world in eighty days. Accompanied by Passepartout, Phineas Fogg completes his journey just in time to win the bet after many fantastic adventures.

How did Mark Twain get his name?

Mark Twain is not the real name of the famous American writer, who lived from 1835 to 1910 and wrote *Tom Sawyer* and *Huckleberry Finn*. His real name was Samuel Clemens. He once piloted steamboats on the Mississippi River, and took his pen name from the call of the men sounding the depth of water. When it was two fathoms deep, they called out 'Mark twain'.

Why is a mean person sometimes called a scrooge?

The word scrooge comes from the book *A Christmas Carol* by the British writer Charles Dickens, which was published in 1843. In this story, an old miser called Ebenezer Scrooge refuses to help the poor and to enjoy himself at Christmas. This is why a mean person is now sometimes called a scrooge. However, the story has a happy ending, as Scrooge is converted to goodness through his encounters with a series of ghosts.

Who was Moby Dick?

Moby Dick is the title of a novel by the American author Herman Melville. It was written in 1851. Moby Dick is the name of a great white whale that is pursued by Captain Ahab and the crew of the whaling ship *Pequod*.

Why did King Arthur have a round table?

In the legends of King Arthur, he and his knights meet at a huge round table with enough space to seat 150. The table is round so that the knights will not be able to argue about which of them should have the most important seats. All the seats are of equal importance at a round table.

Who was Victor Hugo?

Victor-Marie Hugo was a French poet. He is the most famous, and possibly the greatest, of all French poets. As well as poems he wrote dramas and novels including *Notre-Dame de Paris* and *Les Misérables*. He died in 1895.

The great white whale, Moby Dick, and the harpooners of the Pequod

Dance

Who founded the Ballets Russes?

The Ballets Russes (Russian Ballet) was the most famous of all ballet companies. It was founded by Serge Diaghilev who lived from 1872 to 1929, and toured Europe and America with great success from 1909 until the 1930s. Diaghilev brought talented dancers, such as Nijinsky and Pavlova, together with excellent choreographers such as Fokine and Massine and great composers, such as Ravel and Stravinsky.

The five positions in classical ballet

First   Second   Third

Fourth   Fifth

How many basic positions are there in ballet?

The best-known ballets, such as *Giselle*, *Coppelia*, *Swan Lake*, *The Sleeping Beauty* and *The Nutcracker*, are all danced in a similar style of dancing. This is called the classical style, and it is based on certain positions of the feet. These are the positions in which the dancer places the feet as he or she dances. There are in fact five different positions, but many different steps and movements are made with them.

How do ballet dancers turn without becoming giddy?

As they dance, ballet dancers often make several turns in rapid succession. They prevent themselves from getting giddy by turning the head in a different way to the body. The body turns smoothly, but the head is held still for a while and then jerked quickly around. In this way, the head is still most of the time, and the dancer does not become giddy.

Who wrote the ballet *Swan Lake*?

Swan Lake is one of the best-known ballets and is often performed today. The music is by the Russian composer Peter Tchaikovsky, and it was composed in 1876.

A scene from Swan Lake

Who creates the movements of the dancers in a ballet?

Just as someone composes the music for a ballet, another person has to work out the movements of the dancers. This person is called the choreographer. He or she may try to create a story in the dancing. The choreographer will work with the composer if the ballet is a new one. However, many choreographers create a new ballet to existing music, and they may devise a new choreography (new movements) for an old ballet.

Theatre, Film and Television

What is an amphitheatre?

An amphitheatre is a theatre in which the audience does not sit in front of the actors, but surrounds them on all sides. It is a building or an open-air theatre with an arena surrounded by rising rows of seats. The ancient Romans built amphitheatres for entertainments. The best-known is the Colosseum in Rome.

The Colosseum, Rome

Which French playwright died while playing an 'imaginary invalid' in his own play?

This was the playwright Molière, the greatest French writer of comedy. Molière's real name was Jean-Baptiste Poquelin, and he lived from 1622 to 1673. His last play, *Le Malade Imaginaire* (The Imaginary Invalid) was one of his funniest. Molière played the title role of the imaginary invalid, a man who pretends to die to find out what people think about him. It is ironic that Molière died while playing this role shortly after the play opened.

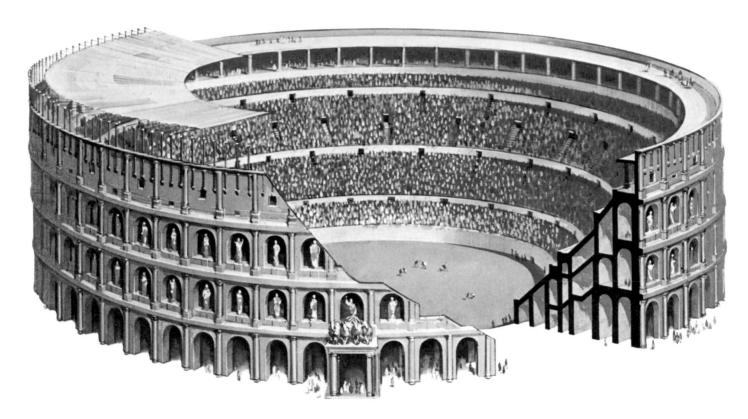

What are props?

The props are all the objects used in a play, a film or a television production. They may be things that the actors hold, such as swords or guns, or they may be objects on the stage, such as furniture, clocks, pictures and so on. The word props is short for 'properties'. In most productions there is someone who looks after the props.

What is a set?

In the theatre, or a film or television studio, the set is the scenery built to resemble a real scene. It is made by carpenters and other workers, and painted and decorated to look like a real room or whatever scene is required for the production. A film studio may build a set outdoors to resemble a whole street or even a small town.

What were miracle plays and mystery plays?

Miracle plays and mystery plays were religious plays that were performed in the Middle Ages. Because many people could not read, the churches put on plays that showed scenes from the Bible and the lives of saints. The plays were not only performed in churches. Companies of actors toured towns and cities, performing their plays on carts that served as a stage.

What is the difference between a producer and a director?

The producer of a play, film or television programme is the person who is in charge of it. He or she has to organize everything that is required to make a production possible. The producer may also decide which production is to be performed, and may have to find the money to pay for it. The director is in charge of the actors and actresses. He or she rehearses them, and tells them how they should act. In films and television, the director also directs the camera operators

How do films and television pictures move?

When you look at a film in the cinema or a programme on a television set, you are not watching a scene that moves continuously. You are actually watching a series of still pictures that flash by very quickly. The film or television camera takes several frames or pictures of the scene every second – usually at the rate of 24 a second in the cinema and 25 or 30 a second in television. The pictures go by so fast on the screen that your eyes do not separate them into single pictures, and you see a scene in continuous motion.

The famous mime artist Marcel Marceau

Which kind of acting does not use words?

Mime or miming is the art of acting without using the voice. The mime puts across a feeling or an action by the expression on the face and movements of the hands and body. A good mime can tell a complete story in this way. Mime is important in ballet, where the dancers cannot speak. It is also a good entertainment in itself, and some actors and actresses give only mime performances.

How is a cartoon made?

A cartoon, or an animated film, is made by drawing or painting every picture or frame separately. When the film is shown, the drawings or paintings appear to move. It takes a long time to make a cartoon. For a ten-minute cartoon, nearly 15,000 separate pictures must be made.

Cartoons are made from a series of drawings.

Why do actors and actresses use make-up?

The lights over the stage in a theatre are so bright that actors and actresses would look pale without make-up. They may also use make-up to change their appearance, for example to make them look older, and they may put on wigs and false noses to look completely different. Make-up is also used in films and television.

Walt Disney and Mickey Mouse

What is a production made on location?

Most films and many television productions are not made entirely in a studio. The cameras, actors and actresses go to a real place and use that to make the film or programme. The place is called a location, and the production is 'made on location'.

Charlie Chaplin

Who made the cartoon films *Snow White* and *101 Dalmatians*?

These famous cartoons, and many others, were made by the American film producer Walt Disney, who lived from 1901 to 1966. Walt Disney became famous for his short cartoons of Mickey Mouse and Donald Duck. *Snow White and the Seven Dwarfs* and *101 Dalmatians* are among his long cartoons, which also include *Bambi*, *Pinocchio* and *Fantasia*.

What was the first film?

Several inventors were involved in the development of films, and it is difficult to say who made the first one. However, the first film to be shown on a screen to the public, as in a cinema today, was made by Auguste and Louis Lumière. These French brothers made a film of workers leaving their factory, and showed it to the public in Paris in 1895. Another Lumière film of a train was so good that people ran away from the screen, thinking it was real.

Which film star appeared in a bowler hat and baggy trousers, and carried a cane?

This strange dress was used by the film actor Charlie Chaplin, who lived from 1889 to 1977, and spent most of his life in the United States. Chaplin made many comedy films in which he always appeared as a tramp dressed in this way. The films were mostly made before sound films were invented, and Charlie does not speak in them. However, the things that happen to him in the films are so funny that people still enjoy them.

SPORT

Who was Babe Ruth?

Babe was the nickname of George Herman Ruth, a famous American baseball player. He began playing with the Boston Red Sox in 1914 when he was 19 years old. When he gave up playing in 1935, he had hit a record total of 714 home runs. This record was not broken until almost 40 years later. Babe Ruth is said to have earned more than a million dollars playing baseball. He died in 1948.

Why does Slammin' Sam Snead deserve his nickname?

Samuel Jackson Snead, an American professional golfer, was given the nickname 'Slammin' Sam' because of his exciting style of playing. He has been described as one of the most naturally gifted players that golf has ever known. Slammin' Sam won more than 130 tournaments and every major championship in which he took part, except one – the US Open Championship.

Who held the world heavyweight boxing title for the longest time?

Joe Louis, an American boxer, was heavyweight champion of the world longer than anyone else. He held the title for nearly 12 years, from 1937 to 1949. He defended his title successfully 25 times and retired undefeated in 1949. He soon returned to boxing because he was short of money, but lost his title to Ezzard Charles. In 1951, he was knocked out by Rocky Marciano and retired. He died in 1981.

Who is Pelé?

Pelé is the nickname of Edson Arantes do Nascimento, a Brazilian association football player. He is considered to have been one of the greatest forwards ever. He was only 17 when he scored twice for Brazil in the World Cup final in 1958. He also played in Brazil's winning teams in 1962 and 1970. By 1969, when he scored his thousandth goal in his 909th match, Pelé had scored an average of more than one goal for every match that he had played. Sometimes called *Perola Negra* (Black Pearl), he became a Brazilian national hero.

Pelé, the Brazilian football player

Who was W. G. Grace?

Dr William Gilbert Grace was a British cricketer. He is one of the best known of all cricketers, and continued playing first-class cricket until he was more than 60 years old. During his career, Grace made 54,904 runs, including 126 centuries. He took 2876 wickets and held 877 catches. He died in 1915.

W. G. Grace

In which sport was Rocky Marciano unbeatable?

Rocky Marciano was unbeatable at boxing. When he retired in 1956, he had fought 49 professional fights and won every one of them. In 1952 he won the world heavyweight title. He defended this title six times, but none of his challengers was able to beat him. He was killed in an air crash in 1969.

How many winners has Willie Shoemaker ridden?

William Shoemaker, the American jockey, is the most successful jockey in the world. Between 1949 and 1990, he rode 8833 winners and is believed to have won more than 103 million dollars. In 1953, his best year, he won 485 races – an average of more than nine wins every week.

In which game was Joe Davis a champion?

Joe Davis was a champion in both billiards and snooker. He held the world snooker championship for a period of 20 years from 1927 until 1946. He was also world billiards champion from 1928 until 1933. During his career in snooker he scored 689 century breaks; that is, he scored at least 100 points in one turn 689 times! Davis died in 1978.

In which sport is Hans-Günter Winkler a leader?

Hans-Günter Winkler is a West German horseman. He has the most outstanding record of any show jumper in international competition. He has won five Olympic gold medals, the Men's World Championship twice, and the European Championship once. He has also taken part in more than 70 Prix des Nations (international team jumping competitions).

Which champion horse won the Grand National the most times?

Red Rum is the only horse so far to have won the Grand National Steeplechase at Aintree, near Liverpool, England, three times. He won in 1973, 1974 and 1977, and came second in 1975 and 1976. Red Rum was born and bred in Ireland and he was trained at a stable in Lancashire. After retiring from racing, he became a celebrity!

Red Rum

Bob Beamon, long jumper

How far did Bob Beamon jump in 1968?

At the Mexico Olympics in 1968, the American long jumper Robert Beamon jumped an amazing 8.9 metres. This jump added 55.25 centimetres to the previous world record, a greater amount than all the additions for the previous 40 years put together! Beamon's record lasted until 1991, when it was beaten by Michael Powell of the USA.

Who first flew a balloon across the Atlantic Ocean?

Americans Ben Abruzzo, Maxie Anderson and Larry Newman were the crew of the first balloon to cross the Atlantic Ocean. Their helium-filled balloon, *Double Eagle II*, left Maine, United States, on 12 August 1978, and landed in Miserey, France, on 17 August after travelling 5001 kilometres. The first crossing in a hot-air balloon was in July 1987 by Richard Branson and Per Lindstrand.

Who was the first person to win all four of the major lawn tennis championships?

Frederick John Perry, a British-born tennis player, was the first person to win all four of the world's major championships. The competitions are the Wimbledon tournament, and the United States, Australian and French Open championships. Fred Perry won the Wimbledon title three times in succession – 1934, 1935 and 1936.

Which team has won the World Cup most times?

Brazil, Italy and the former West Germany: all three times. Brazil won in 1958, 1962 and 1970, Italy won in 1934, 1938 and 1982, West Germany won in 1954, 1974 and 1990. The competition, which takes place every four years, is organized by FIFA which stands for the Fédération Internationale de Football Association.

Why do athletes remember Paavo Nurmi?

Paavo Nurmi, a Finnish athlete, is remembered by athletes because many regard him as the greatest distance runner ever. He held more than twenty world records. Nurmi won nine Olympic gold medals and three silver medals. He used to run with a stopwatch in his hand to check his own speed. At the 1924 Paris Olympics, he ran seven races in six days and won them all. He was known as the 'Phantom Finn'. He died in 1973.

Who was Jesse Owens?

Jesse Owens was one of the greatest track and field athletes the world has ever known. The record that he set for the long jump was not beaten for 25 years. He set six world records in one afternoon in 1935. At the Berlin Olympics in 1936, he won four gold medals. He died in 1980.

Jesse Owens at the Berlin Olympics, 1936

Who were the champion Olympic men's hockey team from 1928 until 1960?

India won the men's hockey championship in every Olympic Games from 1928, when hockey was reintroduced into the Games, until 1960, when they were beaten by Pakistan. In 1964 and 1980 they won again, making a total of eight gold medals.

Which country first defeated Japan in the karate world championship?

Great Britain was the first country ever to beat Japan in international karate competition. Great Britain has won the world team championship six times (1975, 1982, 1984, 1986, 1988 and 1990).

How many gold medals did Mark Spitz win for swimming at the 1972 Olympic Games?

At the 1972 Munich Olympics, the American swimmer Mark Spitz won seven gold medals. He had already won two at the 1968 Mexico Olympics so, with a total of nine, he holds more gold medals than any other male swimmer.

What has Cambridge won more often than Oxford?

Every year, the universities of Oxford and Cambridge compete in a boat race on the river Thames in London. Since 1829, there have been 137 races. Cambridge has won 69 times, Oxford 67 times, and there was a dead heat in 1877.

Who are the Harlem Globe Trotters?

The Harlem Globe Trotters are an American all-black professional basketball troupe. The Globe Trotters were formed in 1927 and became famous for their great skill as well as their amusing performances. They have played before more than 75 million people in 90 different countries.

The Harlem Globe Trotters

How successful has the United States Olympic team been at basketball?

Very. The United States Olympic basketball team won all seven Olympic titles from 1936, when the game was first included in the Olympics, until 1968. The team had won a total of 63 consecutive matches when it lost 50–51 to the Russian team in the Munich Olympics in 1972. There was a dispute, and the Russians won the final after extra time. The United States regained the title in 1976, did not take part in the 1980 Olympics, and won the title again in 1984. However, it failed to win the 1988 title, which went to the USSR.

In which sport did Juan Manuel Fangio y Cia excel?

Usually known as Juan Fangio, he was an Argentinian motor-racing driver. He won the World Drivers' Championship five times, and won 24 Grand Prix races. He retired from motor racing in 1958 when he was 47 years old.

The Rules of Sport

How long is the Tour de France cycle race?

The Tour de France cycle race is about 4000 kilometres long. It is not exactly the same distance every year. It takes place over three weeks, and there are twenty separate stages. The longest race ever held was in 1926, when it covered 5745 kilometres.

Tour de France

In which sports would you find a flyweight?

In boxing and in weightlifting, there is a class of competitor called a flyweight. It is usually the lightest class. In boxing, a flyweight must not weigh more than 51 kilograms. In Olympic and international weightlifting, a flyweight must not weigh more than 52 kilograms.

How many events make up a decathlon?

The decathlon, which is for men only, has ten events: 100 metre, 400 metre and 1500 metre runs, 110 metre hurdles, javelin and discus throws, shot put, high jump, long jump and pole vault. The word comes from Greek words meaning ten and contest, but the decathlon was not a contest in ancient Greece.

Which events make up a heptathlon?

The heptathlon is a seven-event athletic contest for women only. The events are: 100 metre hurdle, shot put, high jump, long jump, javelin, 200 metre run and 800 metre run. The name heptathlon comes from Greek words meaning seven contests.

How long is the pole used in pole vaulting?

The pole used in pole vaulting may be any length, according to the rules of the International Amateur Athletic Federation. In a pole vaulting competition, the judge decides on the minimum height to be jumped. The vaulter may attempt to jump any height above the minimum. Modern poles are made of fibre-glass, and the tremendous flexibility of this material has enabled vaulters to jump as high as 6 metres.

Pole vaulting at the Los Angeles Olympics, 1984

What is the difference between an amateur and a professional in sport?

An amateur sportsman or sportswoman is one who takes part in sport purely because he or she enjoys it, and not for any financial reward. In fact, an amateur must not take money, or he or she will not be allowed to take part in amateur sports. A professional is a person who earns his or her living from sport. The Olympic Games are only for amateurs, while many association football players are full-time professionals.

Why is the Marquis of Queensberry remembered in boxing?

The Marquis of Queensberry gave his name to the first rules for modern gloved boxing, which were drawn up in 1867. The rules were drafted by John Chambers under the name and patronage of John Sholto Douglas, eighth Marquis of Queensberry and they are therefore known as the Queensberry Rules. They state that gloves must be worn, that there are to be rounds of three minutes with one minute's rest between rounds, and that there is to be no wrestling. The Queensberry Rules form the basis of the rules that are applied in boxing today.

What is the difference between rugby league and rugby union football?

The main difference between rugby league and rugby union is that there are thirteen players in a rugby league team and fifteen players in a rugby union team. There are also some differences in the rules and methods of scoring. Rugby union is entirely an amateur game, and rugby league is partly professional.

How many kinds of football are there?

There are at least six different kinds of football. Association football or soccer is probably the most popular kind of football, as it is played in most countries around the world. There are eleven players in each team, and the game is played with a round ball that must not be handled. Rugby football or rugger has thirteen or fifteen players, and the ball is oval and can be carried. American football has eleven players a side and an oval ball that may be carried. Canadian football is like American football, but there are twelve players per team. Australian Rules football is played on an oval pitch, and each side has eighteen players. Gaelic football is like a mixture of soccer and rugger and has fifteen players per team.

American football

Tackling

Punting

What is a formula racing car?

A formula racing car is a car which is built according to rules laid down by a racing authority that state how a car should be designed and what size its engine should be. There are a number of different formulae. The formula one car is designed for Grand Prix races.

McLaren MP4/2B

What is the difference between Alpine skiing and Nordic skiing?

Alpine skiing is downhill skiing and downhill competition. Nordic skiing is a kind of competition that includes cross-country skiing and ski-jumping. Nordic ski racing, called *langlauf*, is a long-distance cross-country ski run. Different kinds of skis are used for Alpine and Nordic skiing.

Alpine skiing in Switzerland

How heavy is the shot used in shot putting?

In shot putting, the shot that is used by men weighs 7.257 kilograms and the one used by women is 4 kilograms. The competitors have to throw the shot from a circle into a special landing area. The object of the sport is to see how far you can put (throw) the shot.

Shot putting

What do swimmers have to do in a medley race?

In a medley race, a swimmer has to swim four stretches of 100 metres, each using one of the four main swimming strokes. The four strokes are freestyle, backstroke, breaststroke and butterfly. Freestyle means that any stroke may be used including the crawl, another high-speed stroke. There is also a medley relay, with teams of four each doing a different stroke.

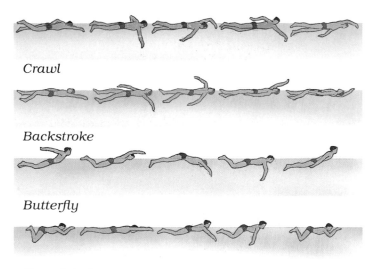

Crawl

Backstroke

Butterfly

Breaststroke

The four main swimming strokes

What happens in curling?

In curling, special large round stones, each weighing about 16 kilograms, are slid across ice towards a target. The stones have handles on them and to help them to move farther, the players sweep the ice in front of the stones with a broom. The game started in Scotland about 500 years ago, but it is now popular in many countries that have cold winters.

What is the difference between a kayak and a Canadian canoe?

A kayak is a very light canoe of the kind used by Eskimos, in which the canoeist uses a double-bladed paddle, one blade for each side. In a Canadian canoe, which is like those used by North American Indians, the paddle has only one blade and there may be one or two canoeists.

In cycling, what is a pursuit race?

In a pursuit race, two riders start on opposite sides of the track. They start at the same time and attempt to catch each other up over a certain distance. Sometimes, in a team pursuit race, the two teams are spaced at regular intervals around the track.

In which sport would you play a chukka?

You would play a chukka in polo. Polo is one of the oldest of all games. It started in Persia in about 500 BC. It is played on horseback, and the ball is hit with a long wooden mallet. A chukka is a period of play in polo. It usually lasts 7 minutes and there are eight chukkas in a game. Chukka comes from a Hindi word, *chakkar*, meaning a round.

Polo

Sporting Terms

In which sport could you find a yorker, a googly and a chinaman?

You could find these odd-sounding things in a game of cricket. They are the names given to certain methods of bowling. A yorker probably gets its name because it was first used by a Yorkshire cricketer. No one knows how a googly was named, but the term is probably Australian. It is thought that a chinaman was named after a Chinese bowler who played for the West Indies, but he was not actually the first player to bowl in this way.

Golfing

Which game is known as ping-pong?

Ping-pong is an old name for the game of table tennis. It was given this name because of the noise the ball makes as it is hit to and fro over the net. The game is like lawn tennis, but is won by the first player scoring 21 points.

In which sport could you make a hole-in-one?

A hole-in-one is a very good score in golf. It means that the player has been able to hit the ball off the tee into the hole with only one (the first) stroke.

How did the Marathon get its name?

It takes its name from the town of Marathon in Greece. It commemorates the run of a messenger called Pheidippides who, in 490 BC, ran from Marathon to Athens, carrying news of an Athenian victory in battle over the Persians. The distance from Marathon to Athens is about 40 kilometres, but the modern Marathon is 42.195 kilometres.

What happens at a rodeo?

A rodeo is a competition for cowboys. The events at a rodeo include bronco-riding, which is trying to ride a half-tamed horse. There are also contests for bull-riding, calf-roping and steer-wrestling. The most famous rodeo is the Calgary Stampede, held in Calgary, Alberta, Canada, each year.

The cowboy who can stay on his horse the longest is the winner in a bronco-riding competition.

What would you do in a steeplechase?

You would race other people. A steeplechase is a race, usually a horse race, in which there are jumps or other obstacles. The name is supposed to have originated in Ireland in 1803, when a party of fox-hunters decided to race in a straight line towards a distant steeple, and jump over anything that happened to be in their way.

Steeplechasing

What is dressage?

Dressage is a special competition for horse riders. The horse and rider have to perform a certain series of movements in an arena. The rider has to halt the horse, make it pace and do figures and turns. Marks are given not only for the rider's control of the horse, but also for the appearance and condition of the horse. Only very talented horses ridden by talented and dedicated riders reach the highest standards of dressage. The Dressage Bureau of the FEI (Fédération Equestre Internationale) sets the rules for judging international competitions.

In which sport would you aim to destroy a skeet?

You would aim to destroy a skeet in clay-pigeon shooting. A skeet is a clay disc which is fired into the air from a trap so that the competitors can shoot at it. It is supposed to look like a bird in flight. The word skeet comes from an old Scandinavian word meaning to 'shoot'.

In which sport would you use a foil?

The sport of fencing uses three weapons – the foil, the épée and the sabre. Women fence only with the foil but men fence with all three weapons.

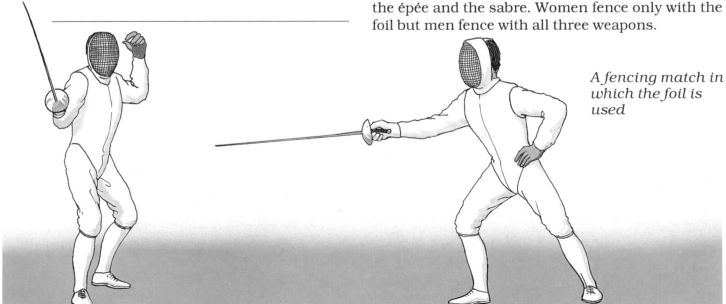

A fencing match in which the foil is used

History of Sport

A judo contest

Which sport was devised by Dr Jigoro Kano?

Judo was devised by Dr Jigoro Kano in Japan in 1882. Dr Kano developed judo from the ancient sport of *ju-jitsu*, a method of self-defence without weapons.

When were the first Olympic Games held?

The very first Olympic Games were held in Olympia, Greece, more than 2000 years ago. It is definitely known that the Games were celebrated in 776 BC, because a record of some of the results has been found. The ancient Games stopped in 393 AD. A Frenchman, Baron Pierre de Coubertin, had the idea of restarting the Olympic Games. The first modern Games were held in Athens, Greece in 1896 and they have been held every four years ever since with the exception of 1916, 1940 and 1944 because of World Wars I and II.

Olympic flag

Where were the Olympic Games held in 1992?

Barcelona, Spain. The Winter Olympics that year were held in Albertville, France.

When were roller skates invented?

The first roller skate was invented in 1760 by Joseph Merlin, of Huy, Belgium. He is supposed to have come sailing into a ballroom on his skates, playing a violin. In 1863, James Plimpton of New York introduced the modern four-wheeled type of roller skate.

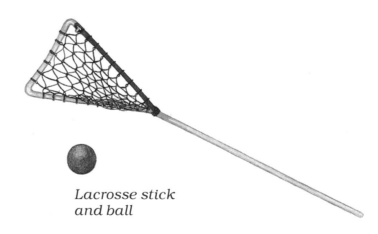

Lacrosse stick and ball

Which modern game was first played by North American Indians?

When French explorers reached Canada in the 1500s, they found the Indians playing the game that we now call lacrosse. This name comes from the French words *la crosse*, meaning 'the crutch'. The *crosse* or stick is a little like a hook with a strong net stretched across it to carry the ball.

Sports Places

What would you do on the Cresta Run?

You would go down the Cresta Run on a toboggan. The Cresta Run is at St Moritz in Switzerland. It is 1212.25 metres long and it drops 157 metres from start to finish. The fastest run so far is 51.34 seconds. This was by Franco Gansser of Switzerland in 1986, when he travelled at an average speed of just over 85 kilometres an hour. People have occasionally reached 145 kilometres an hour!

How big is the largest stadium in the world?

The largest open-air stadium in the world can hold 240,000 spectators and 40,000 gymnasts. It is in Prague, Czechoslovakia. The largest indoor stadium is in New Orleans, Louisiana, United States. It is called the Superdome, and can hold more than 97,000 spectators. It is also the largest dome in the world.

What sport is associated with Wimbledon?

Each year the Lawn Tennis Championship Meeting takes place at Wimbledon in London and players come from all over the world to compete. Croquet also has its headquarters at Wimbledon, but nowadays people immediately think of lawn tennis when they hear the name Wimbledon.

Where are the highest waves for surfing?

The highest waves for surfing, or surf riding, are thought to be those at Makaha Beach, Hawaii. They sometimes reach a height of 9 to 10 metres, which is the highest that people can ride in safety.

Which sport is Monte Carlo famous for?

Monte Carlo is a resort in Monaco on the Riviera renowned for its annual motor rally.

Where would you go orienteering?

You would go almost anywhere on land. Orienteering, which started in Scandinavia, is a combination of walking, cross-country running, and finding your way about the country by using maps and compasses. In competition, it is often played in two teams of eight, but it can be played in pairs. It is a sport enjoyed by people of all ages.

Which sport is enjoyed at Newport?

The most famous of all sailing events, the America's Cup usually takes place off Newport, Rhode Island, United States. A sea race to Bermuda also starts there. Some important deep-sea fishing as well as some major American lawn tennis championships are also held at Newport.

Huge yachts like Australia *sail in the America's Cup.*

WHO?

Who said 'Father, I cannot tell a lie'?

This famous phrase is supposed to have been said by George Washington, the first President of the United States, when he was a boy. He is said to have chopped down his father's cherry tree and, when asked who had done it, he confessed, saying 'Father, I cannot tell a lie'.

Who stole the golden fleece?

The story of the golden fleece is a famous legend of ancient Greece. It was stolen by Jason. The tale is told in the story of *Jason and the Argonauts.*

Which queen is supposed to have said 'Let them eat cake'?

This queen was Marie Antoinette, the wife of King Louis XVI of France. She was not very popular because she was Austrian and also very extravagant. When she was told that the French people were starving and had no bread, she is supposed to have said 'Let them eat cake'.

Which king is supposed to have burned the cakes?

Alfred the Great was King of Wessex (part of southern England) from 871 to about 900. The story is told that while escaping from the Danes, he sheltered unrecognized in a cowherd's hut. He was scolded by the cowherd's wife because he allowed some cakes or loaves to burn!

Who ate the first sandwich?

The sandwich is named after the Earl of Sandwich, who invented this way of eating in the 1700s. He was too busy gambling to stop and eat full meals.

Has anyone ever won the Tour de France more than once?

Yes. Three riders have won the Tour de France cycle race five times each: Jacques Anquetil of France, Eddy Merckx of Belgium and Bernard Hinault of France.

Who was Lenin?

Lenin is the name given to the man who led the Russian Revolution in 1917, and then became leader of Russia. His real name was Vladimir Ilyich Ulyanov.

Who was Pontius Pilate?

Pontius Pilate was the Roman governer of Judaea who ordered the crucifixion of Jesus Christ.

Who was the first person to see both the North Pole and the South Pole?

Few people have been to both ends of the Earth. The first was the Norwegian explorer Roald Amundsen.

Who built the first diving suit?

The first diving suit was a wooden barrel with holes for the diver's arms to poke out, and a window for him to see. It was built by John Lethbridge, a British inventor, in 1715.

Who was Florence Nightingale?

Florence Nightingale was a British hospital reformer famous for her work in the Crimean War. She established the modern nursing profession. She died in 1910.

Who were the sirens?

The sirens were creatures of Greek legends. They were half women and half birds. The sirens had beautiful voices, and sang to sailors who sailed past their shores. But those who stopped to listen met their deaths.

Who was Omar Khayyám?

He was a Persian poet, astronomer, and mathematician who died about 1123. His most famous poem is the *Rubáiyát.*

Who was Cyclops?

In Greek legends, a Cyclops was any one of a group of giants known as the Cyclopes. These were fearsome giants, who had only one eye in the middle of their foreheads.

Who were Zeus and Jupiter?

Zeus and Jupiter are the names of the kings of the gods in ancient Greek and Roman legends.

Who is said to have fiddled while Rome burned?

The Roman Emperor Nero is said to have fiddled while Rome burned. In AD 64, a large part of Rome burned to the ground. It is possible that Nero ordered the fire to be started, so that he could blame Rome's Christians and kill many of them.

Who was Charles the Bald?

King Charles I of France (AD 823–877), was also the Holy Roman Emperor Charles II. To avoid confusion, he was known as Charles the Bald.

Who sculptured *The Thinker*?

The Thinker is a famous statue made by the French sculptor Auguste Rodin (1840–1917).

Who called themselves the Society of Friends?

The Society of Friends is the name of the religious group known as the Quakers.

Who was the Black Prince?

The Black Prince was the eldest son of King Edward III of England. He was called the Black Prince because he wore black armour in battle.

Who was Django Reinhardt?

Jean-Baptiste (Django) Reinhardt was a Belgian guitarist. He combined gipsy music with jazz influences in a unique way.

Who is Tasmania named after?

It is named after the Dutch explorer Abel Tasman, the first European to reach the island in 1642.

Who was Jack the Ripper?

Jack the Ripper is the name given to a man who is thought to have committed several terrible murders in London in 1888.

Viking longship

Who was Leif Ericson?

He was a Viking explorer who sailed westwards in the 900s and found 'Woodland' and 'Vinland', probably Newfoundland and Maryland.

Who became leader of Cuba after the revolution in 1959?

Fidel Castro became leader of Cuba in 1959. He set up a communist government.

Who wrote the opera *La Bohème*?

Giacomo Puccini, the Italian composer. He also wrote *Tosca* and *Madame Butterfly*.

Who is homo sapiens?

You are! Just as animals and plants have Latin names, so do human beings. All human beings belong to the same species so we have the same Latin name. This is *Homo sapiens*, which means 'wise man'.

Who invented numbers?

Different civilizations invented different ways of counting and used different kinds of numbers. The numbers that we use are called Arabic numerals, but they developed in India in ancient times.

Which country was led by President Tito?

Tito was the President of Yugoslavia. He set up a communist government in 1943, and governed until his death in 1980.

Who is the Flying Dutchman?

The Flying Dutchman is a legendary Dutch sailor who has been cursed and condemned to sail the seas for eternity without ever coming to land. It is also the title of an opera based on this legend by Richard Wagner.

WHAT?

What is a nine days' wonder?

Something is called a nine days' wonder if it causes a great sensation for a short time, and then is quickly forgotten.

What would you do with a harmonium?

You would play it. A harmonium is a musical instrument. It has a keyboard, and pedals that you continually push up and down with your feet. The pedals operate a bellows that supplies air, and the keys admit the air to reeds like those in a mouth-organ or accordian.

What is remembered on Good Friday?

The Crucifixion of Jesus Christ is remembered by Christians on Good Friday. 'Good' used in this way means 'holy'.

What is Morse code?

Morse code is a code for letters and numbers made up of dots and dashes. A is . __ , B is __ . . . , and so on. People send Morse code messages over the radio, a dot being a short sound and a dash being a long sound. You can send Morse code by flashing lights too. The code was invented by the American inventors Samuel Morse and Alfred Vail in about 1838.

What would you do with an oriflamme?

You would wave it or display it. An oriflamme is a kind of flag. The name comes from Latin words meaning 'golden flame'.

What happened to Rip Van Winkle?

Rip Van Winkle is a tale by the American writer Washington Irving. It tells of how Rip falls asleep for twenty years, and wakes up an old man.

What would you do with chopsticks?

You would eat with them. Chopsticks are the two small sticks of wood, ivory or plastic that Eastern people use to eat food.

What is the Great Barrier Reef?

The world's largest coral reef. It lies off the north-eastern coast of Australia.

What was Excalibur?

Excalibur was the name of the great sword belonging to King Arthur in the legends about King Arthur and his knights.

What has an obverse and a reverse?

A coin – these are the names of the two sides. The obverse is the front and the reverse is the back.

Are sunspots dark or bright?

Sunspots are dark patches that appear for a short time on the Sun. Do *not* try to look for them with a telescope, because you will badly damage your eyes. In fact, sunspots are not dark at all. They are very bright, like the rest of the Sun's surface, but not quite as bright. They therefore look dark compared with the rest of the surface.

Are there really seas on the Moon?

Some parts of the Moon are called seas. The seas are in fact huge flat plains on the Moon. Centuries ago, astronomers thought that they were seas and the name stuck.

What is NASA?

NASA is the National Aeronautics and Space Administration. It launches spacecraft and satellites into space from the United States.

Which tree grows taller than any other?

The tallest known trees in the world are the coast redwoods of California in the United States. They grow to heights of 112 metres.

What is made in a blast furnace?

Iron is made in a blast furnace.

What is a Great Dane?

A large, strong dog of German, not Danish, origin. It makes a good guard dog.

What is a gnu?

A gnu, which is pronounced 'new', is a large African antelope, with big curved horns and a long mane. It is also called a wildebeest.

What is an anaconda?

A giant snake found in the swamps and rivers of some South American forests. Anacondas can grow to 9 metres in length.

What does RSVP mean?

RSVP means 'please reply'. The letters are the initials of the French words *répondez s'il vous plaît*, which means 'answer please'. These letters are often found at the bottom of an invitation.

What is a mosaic?

A mosaic is a picture or design made up of many little pieces put together. Since ancient times, people have used mosaics to decorate the floors and walls of buildings. They set coloured pieces of tile or stone into cement to build up the picture or design.

What would you do with basil?

You would pick it, sniff it and eat it. Basil is a fragrant wild flower of the mint family. It is used as a herb in cooking.

Monkey puzzle

What is a monkey puzzle?

A monkey puzzle is another name for the tree known as a Chile pine. Someone once said that it would puzzle even a monkey to climb it.

What is porridge made from?

It is made by boiling oatmeal or oatflakes with water to make a paste, and it is served with milk, cream or salt.

What is Esperanto?

Esperanto is a language invented in 1887 by Dr L. Zamenhof of Warsaw in Poland. It was intended to be a universal language that everyone would learn to speak in addition to their own language.

What would you do in a mistral?

You would shelter from it. The mistral is a strong, cold wind that blows in the south of France.

What would you use an abacus for?

You would use it for adding up. The abacus is popular in Asia as a quick and simple method of making calculations. It has rows of beads on wires that correspond to units, tens, hundreds and so on. By moving the beads up and down the wires to represent numbers, you can add or subtract.

What would you do to a pavane, a polonaise and a polka?

You would dance to them. They are pieces of music composed for the dances of these names.

What is caviar?

Caviar is an expensive food obtained from the eggs of a large freshwater fish called the sturgeon. It is usually black in colour, and tastes salty.

What is ju-jitsu?

Ju-jitsu is a form of wrestling. It developed in Japan as a way of fighting without weapons.

What is similar about a triangle, a tricycle and a tripod?

The answer is three. A triangle has three angles or corners (and three sides), a tricycle has three wheels and a tripod has three legs or feet. Many other words that begin with tri- have something to do with three, because tri- comes from Greek and Latin words meaning 'three'.

What is the difference between port and starboard?

Port and starboard are sailors' names for the sides of a boat. As you face forward towards the bow, port is on your left and starboard on your right. The port side has a red light and the starboard side a green light.

What can be either roman or italic?

Printed letters. Upright letters are roman; *sloping letters are italic*.

Which ancient indoor game gets its name from the Persian word for king?

Chess gets its name from the Persian word *shah*, meaning a king. In chess, the most important piece on the board is the king. The object of the game is to try to capture the other player's king. Chess has been played for at least 1500 years.

Which award is called an Oscar?

An Oscar is given for achievement in the cinema. It is a small bronze statuette. The awards are given by the United States Academy of Motion Picture Arts and Sciences, and were called Oscars because someone exclaimed that they looked like their Uncle Oscar!

What is studied in acoustics?

Sound, particularly the way in which sound waves travel inside buildings. In a hall or theatre with good acoustics, the music or speech is clear and you can hear everything easily.

Which animal lives for only a day?

Young mayflies live in lakes and ponds for months or years, and eventually change into adult mayflies. Then they leave the water, and spend a short but active life in the air. The adult mayfly does not feed. It lives only a few hours, in which time it has to breed and lay eggs in the water.

What is 0K in science?

The coldest temperature possible, which is called absolute zero. Temperature is measured in kelvins (K) in science. Absolute zero is zero kelvins or 0K.

What was the Trojan horse?

Greek legends tell of a clever way the Greeks managed to conquer Troy, a rival city that is now in Turkey. The Greeks had besieged Troy for years, and despaired of ever being able to get into the city. So they built a big hollow wooden horse and concealed some men inside it. The rest departed, leaving the horse outside the city gates. The curious Trojans brought the horse inside and, at night, the Greeks stole out of the horse and opened the city gates to their fellows, who had returned. Then they conquered the city.

Which instrument has a name meaning 'soft-loud'?

This instrument is the pianoforte, which we often simply call a piano for short. The name pianoforte means 'soft-loud' in Italian. The piano developed from the harpsichord, and it got its strange name because, unlike the harpsichord, it can be played loudly or softly depending on how hard you strike the keys.

What is plastic surgery?

An operation to change the appearance is called plastic surgery. It is often done to repair damage to the body, in serious burns, for example.

Would you wear a water moccasin?

No, it is not a shoe, but a poisonous snake.

What kind of animal is a laughing jackass?

It is a bird that has a cry like a laugh. The laughing jackass is also called the kookaburra, and it is found in Australia.

Which is the most common letter of the alphabet?

The most common letter in written English is the letter E.

What was the Holy Roman Empire?

The Holy Roman Empire was a group of small German and neighbouring states that were powerful in the Middle Ages. It was intended to be a second Roman Empire built of Christian states.

What is a bookworm?

A person who reads a lot is often called a bookworm, but there is a small insect called a bookworm which eats holes in books.

Can your doctor cure a cold?

No. The common cold has no cure. Hopefully a cure will be found one day, but no one has yet succeeded.

Which animal makes a pit to trap other animals?

The ant-lion larva (young) traps ants and spiders by digging a pit in sandy soil. It lies in wait, buried at the bottom of the pit. When its victim walks into the pit, the ant-lion throws sand at it. The ant or spider falls down the sides, and the ant-lion seizes it.

What is the difference between a colt and a filly?

A colt is a male horse under the age of four. A filly is a female horse under the age of four.

Which deadly weapon harnesses the power of the Sun?

This weapon is the hydrogen bomb, or thermonuclear weapon. The Sun gets its power by changing atoms of hydrogen into atoms of helium. This produces huge amounts of heat. The hydrogen bomb works in a similar way. It is so powerful that it needs an atomic bomb made of uranium or plutonium to set it off.

Which metals are magnetic?

Only the metals iron, cobalt and nickel, and alloys made of them such as steel, are magnetic. Other metals, such as copper, are not magnetic. However, they can be made magnetic by passing an electric current through them. Magnets made in this way are called electromagnets. They do not stay magnetic when the current is switched off.

What is concrete made of?

Concrete is a mixture of water, aggregate (sand, gravel, crushed rock, etc.) and a binding material such as cement.

What is epilepsy?

Epilepsy is a disorder of the nervous system. Epileptics suffer from spells of unconsciousness and may have convulsions (fits).

What is the Rosetta Stone?

The Rosetta Stone is a black slab that was found in Egypt in 1799. It dates from 195 BC. The stone bears three inscriptions, one in Greek, one in ancient Egyptian writing and one in ancient Egyptian hieroglyphics (picture writing). The three inscriptions all have the same meaning, and they enabled scholars to translate hieroglyphics for the first time.

What relation is a gander to a gosling?

The relation between them is father and child. A gander is a male goose, and a gosling is a young goose.

What is a frogman?

People who dive and swim under water with their own air supply are often called frogmen. They get this name because of the long rubber flippers that they wear. These look like frogs' feet, and frogmen swim in a similar way to frogs.

What are cosmic rays?

Cosmic rays are invisible rays that come from space and strike the Earth.

What is hard water?

Hard water is water which does not lather readily with soap.

What is ESP?

ESP stands for extra-sensory perception, which means telepathy or being able to read people's thoughts. It also includes the power to move or influence things just by thought alone. ESP has never been proved to exist.

What does being 'up a gum tree' mean?

If you say that someone is up a gum tree, you mean that they are in difficulties or having trouble.

In which game is one player a dummy?

The card game called bridge. One player has to show their cards to the other players, and this player is called the dummy.

What does CD stand for?

CD usually means *compact disc.* However, the letters CD on a car stand for *corps diplomatique* (diplomatic corps), which means that the car belongs to the embassy of a foreign country. CD also stands for civil defence, and Cd is the symbol for the chemical element cadmium.

Which language is most widely spoken?

Mandarin or Northern Chinese. About 695 million people throughout north and east central China speak this language.

What would you do with a tam-tam and a tom-tom?

You would play them. A tam-tam is a large gong, which you hit with a mallet. A tom-tom is a drum that is usually beaten with the hands.

Which animal was the first in space?

In 1957, a Russian dog named Laika became the first animal in space. She was launched aboard the second spacecraft ever to make a flight, the satellite Sputnik 2. Sputnik 2 could not return to Earth, and Laika died aboard.

What are the doldrums?

The doldrums are parts of the ocean at the equator where there is often no wind. 'Being in the doldrums' means feeling gloomy or in low spirits.

What will China get back in 1997?

Hong Kong. This part of China became a British colony in the 1800s, and is to return to China in 1997.

What is the population of the world?

In 1991, it was estimated that the population of the world reached 5400 million people. It is expected to grow to 6300 million by the year 2000.

What is a prototype?

A prototype is the first thing of its kind. The first model of an invention is a prototype. The word comes from Greek words meaning 'first' and 'model' or 'figure'.

Which animals have both their eyes on the same side of their head?

Several kinds of fish, called flatfish, have thin, flat bodies and live on the sea-bed. The fish lie on the bottom on their sides, and have both their eyes on one side of their head so that both eyes can look up. Plaice and sole are flatfish.

What is freezing point?

Freezing point is the temperature at which a liquid changes to a solid. It is the same as the melting point of a solid. The freezing point of water is 0°C.

Hippopotamuses

Which mammals live in water?

Many mammals live in water. They can swim and dive, but must come to the surface to breathe. Otters, water voles and hippopotamuses are all at home in rivers and lakes, though they often come ashore. Most seals and sea lions live in the sea, but come ashore to breed. Whales, dolphins and porpoises, dugongs and manatees live in the sea and never come ashore.

What is a geyser?

A geyser is a natural fountain. Every so often hot water and steam suddenly gush from the ground in a great spurt. The hot water and steam come from chambers underground, where hot rocks heat the water. The steam builds up and forces the water up to the surface.

What is being colour-blind like?

A colour-blind person sees colours slightly differently to other people. There are different kinds of colour-blindness. The most common form is red-green blindness, which makes it difficult for people to tell red from green. Men have colour-blindness much more than women.

What is a wisdom tooth?

An adult may have four wisdom teeth. They are the teeth at the ends of both rows of teeth. The wisdom teeth are the very last teeth to grow. They do not appear until a person is fully-grown, and supposed to be wise.

Which languages are written in St Cyril's alphabet?

Russian, Bulgarian and Serbo-Croat are written in an alphabet that was invented by St Cyril in about AD 860. The alphabet is called the Cyrillic alphabet, and it has 32 letters, which are similar to Greek letters.

What happens when you cough?

You cough when something, such as smoke or mucus, irritates the throat or bronchial passages, or when they have been inflamed by germs. You try to breathe out while your vocal cords are closed. This raises the pressure of the air, which explodes out when the cords finally open, helping to clear the passages.

Which alphabet begins with the letter alpha?

The Greek alphabet begins with the letter alpha. In fact, the word alphabet comes from the first two Greek letters: *alpha beta*.

What are the Old World and the New World?

After the discovery of America by Columbus, people in Europe realized that a great new continent lay across the Atlantic Ocean. This continent was called the New World, and it consists of North, Central and South America. The rest of the world then known – Europe, Asia and Africa – was called the Old World.

What is soap made of?

Soap is made by boiling oil or fats with sodium hydroxide. Soap contains 15–30% water without which it would be hard and brittle.

Do sea serpents exist?

Long ago, sailors told stories of giant serpents that could destroy ships and gobble up their crews. We do not know of any such animal.

What makes drinks fizzy?

Fizzy drinks contain a gas called carbon dioxide. It is dissolved in the water in the drink. When the drink is poured out of the bottle, the carbon dioxide leaves the water. It forms bubbles, which make the drink fizzy.

What is spontaneous combustion?

Spontaneous combustion happens when something bursts into flame without being lit or ignited. Haystacks sometimes go up in smoke for this reason. The hay gets so warm inside the stack that it starts to burn of its own accord.

What is a hologram?

A hologram is a three-dimensional image made by laser light. Holograms appear to have depth and solidity as if they were real.

What happens when you sneeze?

You may sneeze when something such as dust or pollen irritates the nasal passages. The glottis – the gap between the vocal cords – stays open all the time. The tongue rises up to block the mouth, so that the air and mucus rush out through the nose helping to clear it.

Which fish shoots at its prey?

Fishes usually have to find their food under water, but the archerfish can shoot down its prey above the surface. It lives in rivers and at the shore in Asia. The fish spies an insect, spider or caterpillar clinging to a plant above the water. It then swims up to the surface, pokes out its mouth, and spits a jet of water at its victim. This knocks the prey into the water, where the fish can gobble it up.

What would you do with claret?

You would drink it. Claret is a kind of red wine.

What is a grand opera?

A grand opera is an opera in which every word is sung – even lines that sound like people speaking. In other kinds of opera, these lines are spoken and not sung.

What famous invention was made with a tin can?

The hovercraft was invented with a tin can. In 1954, the British inventor Sir Christopher Cockerell fixed a vacuum cleaner to a tin can to find out if a craft could be made to hover on water. The experiment worked, and Cockerell began to build the first hovercraft.

What is the difference between a stoat and a weasel?

Stoats and weasels are small furry animals with short legs and long tails. They hunt mice, rats and other small animals. Both stoats and weasels are normally brown and white, though they may both go white in winter. The only big difference between them is that a stoat is larger than a weasel. However, in North America there is no difference as all these animals are called weasels.

What is the Venus de Milo?

The Venus de Milo is a famous statue of the goddess Venus. It was carved in ancient Greece in about 100 BC, and it is of white marble. It was found in a cave on the Greek island of Milos (Milo in Italian) in 1820.

What is an oracle?

An oracle is someone who foretells the future.

What was unusual about the god Janus?

Janus was a Roman god, and was unusual because he was shown as having two faces. This was because Janus was the god of doors and gateways, and he had to see both inside and outside at the same time. January is named after Janus because it marks the entrance to the new year.

Are there vampires?

Horror stories and legends abound with tales of vampires, which are ghosts that bite sleeping people and drink their blood. Vampires do not exist in real life, but the idea probably comes from the vampire bat. This is a bat that feeds by sucking blood from sleeping animals, and it has been known to attack sleeping people – without even waking them!

What does goodbye mean?

'Goodbye' is short for 'God be with you'. People used to say the whole phrase once upon a time, but it became shortened.

What is a numismatist?

A numismatist is a person who collects money, particularly coins, and medals. The name comes from the Latin word *numisma*, which means 'a coin'.

What does 'playing possum' mean?

'Playing possum' means pretending to be asleep or dead. We do it to play a joke on someone, but in nature, many animals sham death seriously. They do it if they are caught by an animal like a dog that will not eat carrion (animals that are already dead). They convince their enemy that they are dead, and are left alone. The possum or opossum, a small furry creature found in America, is famous for this trick.

What would you use TNT for?

You would use TNT to blow something up, for it is a powerful explosive. The letters stand for *tri-nitro-toluene*, which is the chemical name of the explosive.

What are binary numbers?

Binary numbers are the numbers that computers use to do calculations. They convert ordinary numbers into binary numbers and back again. Instead of having ten different numbers like ordinary numbers, binary numbers have only two. These are usually shown as 0 and 1. In computers, the numbers are made up of pulses of electricity. 0 is when the current is off, and 1 is when it is on.

What does a red cross mean?

In wartime, a red cross on the side of a vehicle or building shows that it is being used to care for sick and wounded people. Ambulances and hospitals are marked with red crosses in the hope that the enemy will not attack them. A red cross is also the symbol of the International Red Cross, a world-wide organization that gives medical care and does rescue work wherever it is needed.

What are parasite animals?

Parasite animals are animals that need another animal, called a host, to help them survive. Tiny protozoans and worms may live inside other animals, feeding on their bodies or on their food and often causing them harm. Some parasites use their hosts to raise their young. Parasite birds like the cuckoo lay their eggs in the nests of other birds and some insects lay their eggs in animals.

What happened to Narcissus?

In Greek legend, Narcissus was a beautiful youth who fell in love with his own reflection. He could not tear himself away from the pool in which he gazed adoringly at his own image, and he eventually changed into a flower.

What does a philatelist do?

A philatelist collects and studies postage stamps, postmarks and stamped envelopes.

Do unicorns exist?

The unicorn is an animal that exists only in legends. It looks like a horse, but has a single long horn jutting from its forehead.

Unicorn

What was the mystery of the *Mary Celeste*?

The *Mary Celeste* was a sailing ship which was found drifting in the Atlantic Ocean between the Azores and Portugal in 1872. The ship's boat, some equipment, the register and the crew were missing, and no trace of them was ever found. There was nothing wrong with the ship, and no clue to what had happened on board. The mystery of the *Mary Celeste* has never been solved.

What is a cacophony?

A cacophony is a dreadful noise. It comes from two Greek words meaning 'bad sounds'.

What is an aardvark?

An aardvark is a large animal, about the size of a fully-grown man, that looks like a long pig. It lives in Africa, and burrows into the ground in search of termites.

What is a Portuguese man-of-war?

A Portuguese man-of-war is a large jellyfish. It has very long tentacles, which may be up to about 25 metres long. These tentacles have poisonous stings that are dangerous to swimmers.

What is the national emblem of Ireland?

The shamrock is the emblem of Ireland because it was used by St Patrick, the patron saint of Ireland, to teach people about the Holy Trinity. The three leaves represent God the Father, God the Son and God the Holy Spirit. The stem represents one God.

What is measured in reams?

Sheets of paper are measured in reams. A ream is equal to 20 quires of paper, and a quire is 24 or 25 sheets. A ream is therefore equal to 480 or 500 sheets, but it may also be 516 sheets.

Which animal has a name meaning 'wild man'?

This animal is the orang-utan, an ape that lives in the forests of Borneo and Sumatra. Orang-utans look rather like old men, and their name is Malay for 'wild man' or 'man of the forests'.

WHERE?

Where is the loneliest place man has ever been?

The loneliest place anywhere is the far side of the Moon. During all the Moon landings, one astronaut remained in space orbiting the Moon. When he was on the far side of the Moon, he was about 5600 kilometres away around the Moon from his fellow human beings – farther than the distance from London to New York. No one had ever been this far away from other people before, or has been since the Moon landings.

Where do people pay with crowns?

The crown is the unit of currency in Czechoslovakia, Denmark, Iceland, Norway and Sweden.

Where is Llanfairpwllgwyngyllgogerychwyrndrobwllllantysiliogogogoch?

Llanfairpwllgwyngyllgogerychwyrndrobwllllantysiliogogogoch is the name of a small town in Wales. It has 58 letters, and is the longest place-name in Britain. It means St Mary's Church in a Hollow of White Hazel Trees near the Rapid Whirlpool by the Red Cave of the Church of St Tysilio. It is usually called Llanfair P.G. for short.

Does lightning ever strike in the same place twice?

Lightning often strikes in the same place twice or even more times. A flash of lightning comes from the sky, and it usually strikes high objects, like buildings and trees. (This is why you should never shelter under a tree during a thunderstorm). Whenever a thunderstorm occurs, lightning is very likely to strike the same high objects.

Where was the Garden of Eden?

According to the Bible, God placed Adam and Eve in the Garden of Eden. The Garden was a paradise. People who believe that Adam and Eve did exist think that the Garden of Eden could have been between the Tigris and Euphrates rivers, in present-day Iraq.

Where could you see a tablecloth in the sky?

At Cape Town in South Africa. This city is overlooked by Table Mountain, which gets its name because it has a flat top. A cloud floating over Table Mountain is known as a tablecloth.

Where do the Walloons live?

The Walloons live in Belgium. They are the French-speaking people of Belgium. The other people in Belgium speak Flemish, which is similar to Dutch.

Where is Spa?

Several towns have Spa in their names or are called spas; a spa is a place where there are springs of water that people consider to be health-giving. They are all named after a town in Belgium called Spa, which is famous for its springs.

Where would you meet a Maori?

You would be most likely to meet a Maori in New Zealand. The Maoris are the people who lived in New Zealand before settlers came from Europe. Today, about 8% of the people living in New Zealand are Maoris.

Where would you see the Star of Africa?

You can see the Star of Africa in the crown jewels at the Tower of London. There are in fact two Stars of Africa, and they are both huge diamonds. They were cut from the Cullinan diamond, the largest diamond ever found. The smaller Star of Africa is in the Imperial State Crown worn by the king or queen of Great Britain. The larger Star of Africa is in the Royal Sceptre.

Where was the Gold Coast?

The Gold Coast was in Africa. It was the name of a British colony which became a part of Ghana in 1957.

Where is the Appian Way?

The Appian Way is a famous Roman road in Italy. It runs from Rome to the port of Brindisi. The road was built in about 300 BC, and parts of it are still in use today.

Where does east suddenly change to west?

This happens at the Greenwich meridian, which is 0° longitude. This meridian is the line on a map or globe that separates the eastern hemisphere from the western hemisphere. If you cross it, you go from east to west – or west to east. The line is called the Greenwich meridian because it passes through Greenwich in London.

Where is Shangri La?

Shangri La is a name for an ideal place where everything is perfect. It comes from a book by the British writer James Hilton called *Lost Horizon*.

Where would you find a billabong?

You would find a billabong in Australia. It is an aboriginal name for a branch of a river, especially one that forms a pool that may dry up. The word is known from the famous song *Waltzing Matilda*, which starts 'Once a jolly swagman camped by a billabong'.

Where did the pied piper play?

The pied piper played in the city of Hamelin, now Hameln in West Germany. According to an old legend, the pied piper enchanted all the children in Hamelin with his playing. He led them away from the town because he had been cheated by the town leaders.

Where would you find a peninsula?

You would find a peninsula sticking out into water. It is a narrow piece of land that juts out into the sea or a lake so that it is almost entirely surrounded by water.

Where is the kimono worn?

The kimono is worn in Japan. It is a loose coat or robe with wide sleeves and tied with a sash. The kimono is a traditional garment, and it may be worn by men or women.

Where would you come across a dingo?

You would find a dingo in Australia. It is the Australian name for a wild dog.

Which city was once called 'the forbidden city'?

Lhasa, the capital of Tibet (now part of China) once had this name because its Buddhist leaders refused to let Westerners enter the city.

Where would you see a gondola?

You would see a gondola in the city of Venice in Italy. Venice has no streets, but canals. People get about by boat instead of by car or bus. They hire gondolas like people hire taxis in other cities.

Where might you have had to walk the plank?

You might have been forced to walk the plank if you lived in the time when pirates roamed the seas. Pirates sometimes forced their prisoners to walk along a plank pushed out over the side of the ship. The victim fell into the sea, and was left to drown or be eaten by sharks.

Where would you be if you were in quarantine?

You would be kept apart from other people because you might have a dangerous disease. A ship that arrives in port with a dangerous disease aboard is kept away from the other boats, and is said to be in quarantine.

Where are icebergs found?

Icebergs form where glaciers meet the sea. The two main places where this happens are in the North Atlantic Ocean around Greenland, and in the southern seas around Antarctica.

Where does rubber come from?

There are two kinds of rubber. Natural rubber comes from latex, which is tapped from rubber trees that grow in tropical regions. Artificial rubber is made from chemicals.

Where is the tundra?

The tundra is a region of land in the Arctic. If you go far enough north it gets too cold for trees to grow. The forests stop and land covered with low plants lies ahead. This is the tundra.

Where is the oldest university in the world?

The oldest university is more than 1100 years old. It is the university at Fez in Morocco.

Where would you be if you were in limbo?

If you were in limbo, you would be in a place where nobody would know about you or where you had been forgotten. In some Christian religions, limbo is a place where the souls of children who have not been baptized go if they die.

Which cities were destroyed by a volcano in AD 79?

The volcano Vesuvius near the Bay of Naples in Italy erupted in AD 79 covering the city of Pompeii with thousands of tonnes of cinders and ash killing about 2000 people. The smaller city of Herculaneum was buried by the same eruption.

Where are the Great Lakes?

The Great Lakes are a group of five huge lakes at the border of Canada and the United States. Lake Superior is the largest, and then come Lake Huron, Lake Michigan, Lake Erie and Lake Ontario.

Where is 'the roof of the world'?

'The roof of the world' is a name given to the part of Central Asia where the Himalayas and several other ranges of high mountains meet. It is situated at the borders of China, India, Pakistan and Afghanistan.

Komodo dragon

Are dragons found anywhere?

There are animals called dragons and they look like the dragons of fairy stories. The most fearsome is the Komodo dragon, a huge lizard that lives in Indonesia. It grows to about three metres long, and kills goats, wild pigs, and other large animals with its sharp teeth.

Where are the Thousand Islands?

The Thousand Islands are a group of about 1500 small islands in the St Lawrence River on the border between the United States and Canada.

Where would you see the Plimsoll line?

The Plimsoll line can be seen on the side of any ship. It marks the highest point to which water should come up the side. If water goes above the line, then the ship is overloaded and may capsize.

Which country has the world's oldest parliament?

A parliament is a gathering of people who govern a country. The first parliament that still exists is the Althing in Iceland. It was set up in AD 930. However, it has not governed continuously since then. The oldest continuous parliament is the Tynwald in the Isle of Man in Great Britain. It is about a thousand years old.

Where would you see an autogiro?

Nowadays you would see an autogiro in a museum, but once you would have seen one in the air. The autogiro is a form of helicopter that is no longer used. It has a rotor, like a helicopter, to lift it into the air, but the rotor is not powered by a motor. Instead, a propeller on the front of the autogiro drives it through the air and the rotor spins automatically, lifting it into the air.

Are all the stars great distances apart?

The Sun is a long way from the nearest star. Many stars are not so lonely, having companion stars. They often exist in pairs called double stars. Some stars have formed in groups called clusters. The Pleiades is a star cluster that you can see with the naked eye in northern skies.

Where does energy come from?

Our most important source of energy is the Sun. It gives us light and heat to stay alive. We also get energy by burning fuels such as gas, coal and petrol. Electricity mainly comes from burning fuel. However, the fuels were formed from the remains of plants and animals – and these needed the Sun's energy to live in the first place.

Japan

Canada

USA

Which country has a flag with a red circle on a white background?

This is the flag of Japan. It is a symbol of the Sun in the sky. Japan is sometimes called the 'land of the Rising Sun'.

Which country has a maple leaf on its flag?

Canada's flag has two vertical red bands between which is a white band with a red maple leaf in the centre. The flag was adopted in 1965.

Which country's flag is known as the 'star-spangled banner'?

The flag of the United States is known as the 'star-spangled banner' and also the 'stars and stripes'. In the top left corner, it has a blue panel with fifty stars – one for each of the states. The rest of the flag consists of seven red stripes and six white stripes. These stripes represent the thirteen original states that formed the United States in 1776.

Where did Fletcher Christian quarrel with Captain Bligh?

This famous quarrel took place on the sailing ship *Bounty* in 1789. In 1787, the *Bounty* set sail from England to Tahiti under the command of Captain William Bligh. Captain Bligh was a very harsh captain and, after serving for two years under him, his mate Fletcher Christian led many of the crew in a mutiny against him.

Do mermaids live in the sea?

Mermaids are creatures that are supposed to be half human and half fish. The top half of a mermaid is a beautiful woman, and the bottom half has the tail of a fish. They do not exist, but the stories of mermaids probably come from sailors who saw dugongs or manatees. These creatures are sea mammals, and are fish-like in shape. Their heads are more human in appearance. They live at the shores of tropical oceans.

Where is the Valley of the Kings?

The Valley of the Kings is in Egypt. It is a valley where many pharaohs of ancient Egypt were buried in tombs.

Where was the first full-scale power station using nuclear energy built?

It was built at Calder Hall, Britain, in 1956.

Which countries use francs for money?

The franc is the unit of currency in France, Belgium, Switzerland and Luxembourg. It has the same value in Belgium and Luxembourg, but is worth greater amounts in France and Switzerland. Francs are also used in countries that were once colonies of France and Belgium.

Where is Oxbridge?

It is not anywhere. Oxbridge is the name given to the universities of Oxford and Cambridge. 'Going to Oxbridge' means attending either of these universities.

Would you enjoy being in pandemonium?

You might, but it's unlikely. Pandemonium is a scene of wild disorder, noise and confusion. The word comes from a Greek word meaning 'all demons'.

Which are the biggest and smallest states in the USA?

Alaska is the biggest state and Rhode Island the smallest state. Alaska is 500 times bigger than Rhode Island.

Where was Constantinople, and what is it now?

Constantinople was once the capital of Turkey. It is now called Istanbul, and the capital of Turkey is now Ankara.

Where is the Kremlin?

The Kremlin is an old citadel in the centre of the city of Moscow in Russia. It was formerly the centre of government for the Communist USSR.

WHEN?

When were the Dark Ages and the Middle Ages?

The Middle Ages lasted for about a thousand years after ancient Rome was destroyed in the AD 400s. The fall of Rome marked the end of the ancient period in history. Civilization and learning vanished from Europe until about 1000, and this period of the Middle Ages is called the Dark Ages. However, they remained alive in Arab countries and in Asia. In about 1450, new discoveries began to be made in Europe. This marked the end of the Middle Ages and the beginning of modern times.

When do married couples celebrate their golden wedding?

On the fiftieth anniversary of their wedding day.

When was the submarine invented?

The first craft that is known for certain to have sailed under water was the *Turtle*. The *Turtle* was egg-shaped, and powered by hand. One man sat inside the submarine, and wound handles to drive propellers that moved the *Turtle* forward, backward, up and down. The *Turtle* was built by an American engineer called David Bushnell. In 1776, the *Turtle* went into action against a British warship. It tried to blow up the warship, but failed.

The Turtle was the first submarine.

When was the first nuclear-powered submarine built?

The American nuclear-powered submarine built in 1955 was the first of its kind. It was called *Nautilus*.

Will the Sun ever stop shining?

If the Sun suddenly went out, it would stop producing light and heat. There would be no sunshine, only everlasting night. We could make our own light, but plants would stop growing and we would soon have no food. Even worse, no heat would reach us from the Sun and it would get very cold very quickly. We would probably freeze to death before we starved. However, there's no need to worry about this. The Sun will continue to shine for 5000 million years.

Can you see rainbows at night?

Rainbows can be seen at night. Moonlight will produce a rainbow if it falls on some rain, just as sunlight does during the day. However, a moonlit rainbow is very faint and you cannot make out any colours in it. It looks like a faint white bow in the night sky.

When was the first criminal caught by radio?

In 1910, Dr Hawley Crippen poisoned his wife in London and escaped to the United States aboard an ocean liner. The police found her remains and traced Crippen. They sent a radio message to the liner, and Crippen was arrested.

When was oxygen discovered?

In 1774, an English chemist called Joseph Priestley obtained a new gas in an experiment. He noted that mice became very frisky when breathing the gas. He had discovered oxygen.

When were the Wars of the Roses?

The Wars of the Roses were civil wars fought between the Houses of Lancaster and York in England from 1455 to 1485. They were called the Wars of the Roses because the Lancastrians wore a red rose for a badge and the Yorkists a white rose. The Lancastrians won.

When was dynamite invented?

Dynamite was invented in 1866 by the Swedish inventor Alfred Nobel. This gave tunnel builders a powerful new explosive. Nobel made a fortune from his invention and founded the Nobel prizes.

WHY?

Mongoose

Why do we have leap years?

Every four years, we have a leap year of 366 days instead of 365 days. The extra day is 29 February. The reason is that a year – the time it takes the Earth to go exactly once around the Sun – is not exactly 365 days long. It is actually 365 days 6 hours 9 minutes $9\frac{1}{2}$ seconds. This is just over $365\frac{1}{4}$ days, so we have an extra day every four years to make the year $365\frac{1}{4}$ days long on average. Every year that can be divided by 4 – such as 1992 – is a leap year.

Why do people faint?

If you faint, you lose consciousness. Everything goes black, as if you suddenly fall asleep, and you fall over. You stay like this for a short time, and then come around (wake up) feeling normal. You faint because the blood supply to your brain gets too low. This can happen if you stand still for a long time, or stand up very quicky.

Why do many people wear glasses?

Many people have to wear glasses to see properly. Without them, things look blurred. This happens because the lens (the clear part in the middle of the eye) does not work properly. An extra lens is needed over each eye, so they wear a pair of glass lenses – which we call glasses or spectacles.

Compass

Why does a compass always point north?

A compass is a tiny magnet, and the Earth is a huge magnet. The ends or poles of the Earth's magnet are near the North and South Poles. The compass turns so that one end points towards the North Pole and the other end towards the South Pole. In fact, a compass does not point exactly north, but the difference from true north is very small.

Why could a mongoose be called fearless?

Mongooses are small furry animals that come from Africa and Asia. They are famous for the fearless way in which they attack deadly snakes such as cobras. Before it can strike, the mongoose seizes the snake by its neck and kills it.

Why did people seek the philosopher's stone?

In the Middle Ages, people searched for the philosopher's stone because they thought it would bring them riches. It was not a stone but a substance that the alchemists – the scientists of that time – thought would turn all other metals into gold and silver. Nobody ever found the philosopher's stone – simply because it cannot exist.

Why is May Day a distress call?

Ships and aircraft in danger use the words 'May Day' to call for help over the radio. It is an international distress call. The words probably come from the French words *m'aidez*, meaning 'help me'. These are pronounced like May Day.

Why would you go to a chiropodist?

You would go to a chiropodist to get treatment for your toes, feet or hands.

Why does the goliath beetle have a good name?

The goliath beetle has a good name because it is a giant beetle. It is named after the giant Goliath who, according to the Bible, was killed by David with a stone from a sling. The goliath beetle is in fact the heaviest insect in the world. It weighs as much as 100 grams and lives in central Africa.

HOW?

Does the zodiac affect us?

The zodiac is the belt of twelve constellations of stars through which the Sun appears to move in a year. The Latin names of the constellations are Aries, Taurus, Gemini, Cancer, Leo, Virgo, Libra, Scorpio, Sagittarius, Capricornus, Aquarius and Pisces. Some people believe that the positions of these constellations, particularly at the time of birth, affect your life. Most astronomers do not believe this.

How would you measure the length of a dynasty?

You would measure a dynasty in years. A dynasty is a line of rulers that all belong to the same family. It begins with a new ruler, such as a king or emperor. His descendants become rulers in turn, and the dynasty continues until a ruler has no descendants to follow him or is overthrown. The longest dynasty is that of the emperors of Japan. It started about 2000 years ago, and still exists. The present Emperor, Hirohito, is the 124th Emperor of the dynasty.

How tall can people grow?

Very, very few people have grown taller than 2 metres 50 centimetres, and this is about the limit of growth. People that grow this tall are not normal. They have a gland disorder that makes them grow too much, and they usually die at an early age.

How many are a billion and a trillion?

A billion is usually a thousand million, but it is sometimes used in Britain to mean a million million. This means that a trillion is either a million million, or a million million million, depending on what you mean by a billion.

How many popes have been called John?

Twenty-three. The first was St John who was Pope from AD 523 to AD 526. John XXIII was Pope from 1958 to 1963.

How long can people stay in space?

Nobody knows if people could live in space as long as they do on Earth. Perhaps they could live longer. The longest single spaceflight made so far lasted almost 366 days. Two Russian spacemen made this spaceflight in 1987–1988 and came to no harm. The Russian spaceman Musa Manarov has spent a total of 534 days in space.

How can you make electricity?

You can produce electricity by rubbing a balloon up and down against a fabric such as wool. It will then cling for a time to a surface such as a ceiling because it becomes charged with electricity. This kind of electricity is called static electricity.

How is a steel boat able to float in water?

Metal is heavier than water, so how can a steel boat float? The answer is in the shape of the boat. There is a lot of space inside the boat, and this makes the whole of the boat lighter than the same amount of water. The boat therefore does not sink.

How many volts go through overhead cables?

Electricity comes to our homes from power stations. There, huge generators make the electricity which goes through overhead cables to towns. To lose as little power as possible, the current travels at very high voltages – as high as 765,000 volts. Before the electricity enters our homes, the voltage is lowered in transformers.

How can we get power from water?

In many places, falling water is used to turn the blades of a turbine, just as flowing water once turned water-wheels. The turbine is connected to an electricity generator. Electricity produced in this way is called hydroelectricity. About a sixth of all the world's electricity is generated by falling water.

How many is a baker's dozen?

A dozen is 12, but a baker's dozen is 13! Bakers once gave 13 rolls to people who asked for 12, to make sure that they could not be charged with giving short weight (too little).

Do stars last for ever?

All stars shine by burning the hydrogen gas that they contain. Sooner or later, they use up all this fuel. Astronomers believe that two things may then happen. Smaller stars, like the Sun, swell up and then shed their outer layers and shrink to become a cold dwarf star the size of a planet. Larger stars explode and blow themselves to pieces. A strange body called a neutron star or black hole may be left after the explosion.

How much is a knot?

The speed of a boat is measured in knots. One knot is equal to a speed of one nautical mile an hour. A nautical mile is longer than an ordinary mile. It is equal to 6080 feet or 1853 metres.

Does ivy take food from the tree on which it grows?

No, it only uses the tree to hold itself up.

How heavy is your brain?

About a kilogram. The average weight of an adult brain is 1.4 kilograms for men and 1.3 kilograms for women.

How old are the oldest paintings?

The oldest known paintings were made by pre-historic people in caves. They painted animals and hunters on the walls of their caves as long as 30,000 years ago.

A cave painting from Lascaux, France

How far away is the horizon?

If you stand on the seashore, the horizon (where the sea meets the sky) is about 4 kilometres away. You cannot see beyond this distance because the Earth is round and the sea curves away out of sight. The distance of the horizon depends on how high you are. If you stood on a cliff 30 metres high you could see about 20 kilometres out to sea.

How did Thursday get its name?

Thursday is short for Thor's Day. Thor is the god of thunder in Scandinavian or Norse legends. Thor was considered to be such an important god that a day of the week was named after him in Scandinavian countries. This has come into English as Thursday.

How is the election of a new pope first announced?

People gather at the Vatican in Rome when a new pope is being chosen. There are several ballots, and the result of each one is announced by a puff of smoke from a chimney. If the smoke is black, it means that there has not been a firm result and another ballot must be held. When a new pope is finally elected, a puff of white smoke comes from the chimney.

How were stocks used to punish people?

Stocks were a form of light punishment used until the last century. Wrong-doers were placed in the stocks, which had holes to fasten the feet, and sometimes the hands and neck as well. They were kept in the stocks for several hours or days.

How long was a league?

A league was once a measure of distance. At sea, a league was just over $5\frac{1}{2}$ kilometres. On land, its length varied from one country to another. The league of the ancient Romans was nearly $2\frac{1}{4}$ kilometres, whereas in Spain, a league was nearly 7 kilometres.

How do you interpret the Roman numeral MI?

In Roman numerals, M is a thousand and I is one, so MI is – guess what – 1001!

Index

INDEX

PHOTOGRAPHIC ACKNOWLEDGEMENTS

The publishers wish to thank the following for kindly supplying photographs for this book.

Page 11 American Meteorite Laboratory; 17, 19 NASA; 25 Met Office; 28 ZEFA; 35 *top* United States Travel Service, *bottom* ZEFA; 36 ZEFA; 39 Spectrum; 82 Hughes Aircraft Co; 85, 89 ZEFA; 92 Robert Harding Picture Library; 93 Goodyear; 96, 97 Mansell Collection; 102–104 ZEFA; 109 World Health Organization; 110 ZEFA; 113 Mansell Collection; 116 Press Association; 117 Mansell Collection; 118 British Museum; 120 Mansell Collection; 121 *top* Peter Newark, *bottom* Sonia Halliday Photos; 122 Peter Newark; 124 *top* Mansell Collection, *bottom* Aldus Books; 126 European Parliament, London; 127 ZEFA; 128 Scala; 129 Popperfoto; 130 Bildarchiv Preussischer Kulturbesitz; 132 Osterreichische Nationalbibliothek; 133 Popperfoto; 134 Mansell Collection; 135 *top* National Portrait Gallery, *centre* Mansell Collection; 136 Mansell Collection; 138 Zoë Dominic; 140 BBC Hulton Picture Library; 141 *top* Walt Disney Productions, *bottom* British Film Institute; 142 All-Sport; 143 *top* RTHPL, *bottom* All-Sport; 144, 145 All-Sport; 146 All-Sport; 148 *left* Swiss National Tourist Office, *right* All-Sport; 150 ZEFA; 152 All-Sport; 153 ZEFA; 171 French Government Tourist Office.

Picture Research: Jackie Cookson, Lisa Simmons